THOSE
WHO
LOVE
THE
GAME

Glenn Rivers / Bruce Brooks

THOSE WHO LOVE THE GAME

Glenn "Doc" Rivers on Life in the NBA and Elsewhere

HENRY HOLT AND COMPANY • NEW YORK

Henry Holt and Company, Inc.
Publishers since 1866
115 West 18th Street
New York, New York 10011

Henry Holt is a registered trademark of Henry Holt and Company, Inc.

Published in Canada by Fitzhenry & Whiteside Ltd.,
195 Allstate Parkway, Markham, Ontario L3R 4T8.

Library of Congress Catalog Card Number: 93-80268

ISBN 0-8050-2822-6

First Edition—1993

Printed in the United States of America on acid-free paper. ∞

10 9 8 7 6 5 4 3 2 1

I dedicate this book to my family:
my wife, Kris; my kids,
Jeremiah, Callie, and Austin;
also my mom, dad, and brother, Car;
and to anyone who has been denied
or told he or she couldn't achieve,
and did it anyway.

—Glenn Rivers

Here is one of my favorite poems, G.R.:

I'm tired of sailing by little boat
far inside the harbor bar.
I want to go where the big ships float,
out on the deep where the great ones are.
And should my frail craft prove too slight
for the waves that swoop those billows o'er,
I'd rather go down in a stirring fight
than drown to death on the sheltered shores.

—*Anonymous,* quoted by Jesse Jackson
at the 1988 Democratic National Convention

Contents

Foreword

An old myth about writers says that every one of us has a first novel "in the drawer"—a book written in all earnest but never published, a final dress rehearsal that brought us to the point of our genuine debut, one book later. Like many myths, this one is often true. Every novelist I know has a book in the drawer.

Mine is a coulda-been-a-novel titled *None Dare Call It Speed*. The text is the first-person narrative of a hyper-intellectual white writer who was hired to ghostwrite the autobiography of a cryptic black baseball player named Reed Roosevelt, centerfielder for the New York Yankees. Finding he could not communicate with the weird ballplayer, the writer decided to invent a wonderful character instead and write the book in his fictitious voice, attributed to Reed. That book—called *What Makes Reed Roll?*—became a hit, and the player received all the credit. The talk-show hosts and columnists and English professors never seemed to notice that the cryptic real-life Reed did not match the loquacious narrator he was written out to be: they believed the "autobiography" instead of their eyes and ears. The text of *None Dare Call It Speed*, then, is the bitter writer's attempt to claim his authorship and tell the real story. The end. Pretty neat, huh, with all those layers of text? Nope: into the drawer.

Now, fifteen years and ten books later, I find myself (a hyper-intellectual white writer) in the weirdly foreshadowed position of introducing a *real* book written with a *real* athlete (a black star in New York). The similarities to my unredeemed novel seem striking. So the question is obvious—have I done a literary number on Doc Rivers, and invented a persona in his name, just to fulfill my frustrated destiny?

The answer, thank goodness, is "No!" There are a lot of reasons why not. The best one is Doc Rivers himself. Unlike my fictitious centerfielder, who was tricksy and secretive and strange, Doc is one of those terrific people who notice almost everything, think about almost everything, and can express precisely and honestly how they feel about almost everything. What is more, Doc's feelings add up to a coherent moral take on the world that is a pleasure to represent in words: The wonderful character as written in *this* book is the real fellow, not a clever writer's invention.

Also, basketball—Doc's game—is tremendously different from baseball. Hoops has more quickness, body contact, spontaneity, rhythm, flow, scoring. The *literature* of basketball is nothing like baseball lit either. In my would-be novel, the fictitious writer was just like many living intellectuals who have reinvented baseball in words, as the intricate apotheosis of their refined wits, if not the apotheosis of all human history. For the most part, the folks who write about hoops have no such fabulous pretenses. My favorite basketball books—Bill Russell's *Second Wind*, Bill Bradley's *Life on the Run*, Dave DeBusschere's *The Open Man*—treat the game as if it needs to be nothing more than, simply, a game. A clutch hook shot at the buzzer is interesting enough as a clutch hook shot—it doesn't have to be exalted as a work of art or a social statement.

The last distinction between this book and my phony one is that I am thrilled with the whole process and the book itself, while my fictitious writer was bitter. Doing a book with another person is *not* a sacrifice of authorial initiative or satisfaction. During the research and the writing, I had to use every one of my novelist's "skills"—inquiring, observing, thinking, listening, designing, writing, etc.—but all in the service of telling the truth about a great guy and a great game. Nothing could be more fun. There is less difference than you might think between writing about a fictitious basketball player (as I did in my actual first novel, *The Moves Make the Man*) and a real one: In both cases, a writer feels he has a story about people to relate. Sometimes the people are real, sometimes not. Doc is real, and it has been enlightening to try to deliver his reality to you.

Those Who Love the Game is the product of a team, on which Doc and I are only two of the five starters. Marc Aronson, the book's editor and point guard, came up with the initial idea and got Doc and me together, with the help throughout of Steve Kaufman, Doc's attorney. But the strong, all-guts-no glory rebounder who kept the ball alive much of the time is Kris Rivers, Doc's wife, whose generosity, intelligence, and insight run throughout this book.

—*Bruce Brooks*

THOSE
WHO
LOVE
THE
GAME

*T*hat dunk," says Doc Rivers, shaking his head, "may become the biggest challenge John Starks has ever faced."

Rivers is sitting on the floor of a high-ceilinged room in his home in Connecticut, a room he calls his sanctuary, with John Coltrane's "Naima" sweetening the air in stereo, and eleven-month-old Austin Rivers tooling around the edge of the glass coffee table and gurgling in mono. "That dunk" refers, of course, to the amazing shot Starks threw down over Michael Jordan and Horace Grant in the fourth quarter of Game Two of the 1993 Eastern Conference finals. We have all seen it twenty times; indeed, only a few hours after it ripped the cords it had become a signature shot for The Exciting Game of Pro Basketball, as touted by the NBA itself in those brilliant promotional highlight commercials that seem to run over and over and over on network TV.

The shot went like this: In a close game, on a crucial possession, with the twenty-four-second clock down to about five, Starks drove the baseline, ran into two of the best defenders in the game, rose in a shockingly vertical spring, and tomahawked the ball over them with his left hand. It was a big two points. But it was also one of those rare shots that cuts the heart out of a defense: The Bulls were humiliated, and not even Jordan could shake it off for the remainder of the game.

"You can read that John was deliberate and cunning and ingenious to design such a shot, but the fact is, that dunk came out of pure desperation," Rivers laughs. "John had dribbled into trouble, which is pretty easy to do against the Bulls. I was actually starting back upcourt to set up on D. There was no way he was going to score or we were going to get a rebound—the Bulls had the paint, they had John, they had everything. So—*boom,* out of nothing John creates a bucket. Two points when we needed two points."

Ah, but it quickly became a great deal more than two points. "The trouble is," Rivers says, "the shot was the biggest thing in the world. The shot itself, not the whole game. There were dozens of newspaper articles analyzing it, saying how it symbolized the way the whole series would play out, symbolized the Knicks' arrogance, symbolized Starks's arrival and his potential superiority over Jordan. . . . Any point the writers wanted to make, they could use that shot as an illustration. And they did. It was on television around the clock no matter where you turned—Starks dunking and dunking and dunking. Reporters were all over him and they asked about nothing else. People in the street hollered at him about it— enthusiastically, of course. Man, somewhere there were probably even *posters* being printed. Overnight John was a folk hero: He was literally the biggest star in the NBA in one leap. All for a completely desperate move that he did by instinct in two seconds in the heat of a game."

But the aftermath made it impossible for Starks to see it that simply, Rivers says; John felt he had to consider the very smart-sounding, often elegant explanations of what the shot meant. These interpretations were, after all, words of praise; how can you resist cocking an ear toward someone who says you have just created an act of genius, dense with meaning? A twenty-seven-year-old from Tulsa who was never even drafted by an NBA team is not used to being called a genius by sophisticated New York media types. You tend to listen to those guys a little. You watch the film, like everyone else, and you start to think, "Wow—I really *did* do something. Didn't I?"

Starks thus became—for a brief time, one hopes—the Sonny Rollins of the NBA. In the mid-1950s Rollins blew through the New York jazz scene as The Man on tenor saxophone. No one could touch him for the perfect balance he achieved between rough power and fluid grace, between clever invention and emotional directness, between note and tone. But when his album *Saxophone Colossus* appeared, one of its biggest fans was the director of the New England Conservatory, Gunther Schuller, an art-music composer of prodigious academic power. Schuller wrote an incredibly brilliant analysis of one of Rollins's solos on a song called "Blue Seven," an article that should stand forever as the greatest example of how an intellectual can turn a spontaneous improvisation into an abstract masterpiece through sheer word power. Schuller praised the solo to the heavens for its intricate technical achievements, spelling out all of the dazzling tricks and motifs Rollins "composed," as if Sonny had sweated over the piece for years. The article got very wide play, and Rollins read it. He was flattered to receive such serious treatment. Trouble was, he had not sat around puzzling about how he could invert the harmonic sequence of a flatted fifth for the recapitulation of theme in the third chorus; he had stood up and played a solo that came to him as he blew, in real time. The discrepancy between the deliberateness Schuller attributed to him and the quickness with which he had played made Rollins feel obligated to start observing himself. *Am* I doing all of that? *Am* I inverting the harmonic structure of a flatted fifth? Whew! I better start paying attention. I better start *thinking*. But when he started thinking, Rollins found he couldn't play his horn. The result: He froze up, and lost his gift, and disappeared for two years, playing alone until he got it back.

"You think too much on the basketball floor," says Rivers, "and you're dead. Concentrate, certainly. Play smart, of course. But playing smart usually means making a move too quick for thought—taking a shot or throwing a pass or slapping at the ball by instinct, because you are wrapped up in the game so deep that you don't have time to analyze. That's how John has to play; that's how we all have to play. Even the players the media dub 'super-intelligent' play almost entirely by instinct. You can't watch yourself to see if you're the genius the papers say you are. You've got to *play*."

As Rivers talks, it is clear his real subject is not John Starks and his dunk. Rivers is really looking at the weird discrepancy between the quick game of basketball as played on the court by human beings making snap decisions that are often invisible—and the smooth, shiny, ultravisible realm of NBA basketball as projected by the league and the media, in which the quickness is packaged (without irony) in slow motion, and the snap moves are rendered as if they had been calculated by choreographers. The more the game is taken apart and reassembled in the tape editing room, the less it resembles the game the players play. The more a move is written about by excited, speculative columnists looking for higher meanings, the less it belongs to the man who made it and the moment in which it was made. It is obvious the players' game is the real game, and the public's is a secondary invention. But what may not be so obvious is this: The game is over in forty-eight minutes, but the highlight film and the clever column tend to endure.

The players know this, of course. As long as there have been sportswriters and broadcasters, there have been inventive, complex retellings of simple on-court events. Sometimes this amuses the players, sometimes it angers them. Rivers smiles and mentions a few examples of absurd invention, when journalist confronts jock with a theory and won't take no for an answer, refusing to hear anything but details that confirm his hypothesis.

"You'll get a writer telling you that you thought something you didn't think, or even did something you didn't do," says Rivers. "*Insisting* on it. 'In the first quarter you were trying to intimidate so-and-so.' 'No, I had no intention of doing that—I was just feeling quick and hitting that short jumper, so I took it.' 'No, you were trying to embarrass him.' 'No—as a matter of fact, that's the last thing I would do, because when *that* guy gets embarrassed, he gets angry and plays better, so I didn't—' 'No, that's wrong! You were trying to intimidate him! It was obvious!' And so on." Rivers shakes his head and watches Austin, who is disassembling a CD jewel box. "I pretty much like the writers and media people. I understand their predicament—their job is to find something new to write about in each game, when in fact all eighty-two games are basically the same. And they have to do it by tomorrow! It's a hard job. But some of them can be like kids—they won't listen, because they know everything. It can be pretty funny."

But it doesn't always stop at being funny. Because ultimately the columns get into print, the edited tapes go out over the air, and the weird ideas are pushed before the public despite the fact that they are fiction and fantasy. The players, meanwhile, cannot live the fiction; they cannot step into the fantasy. They have to play the real game, night after night, against real opponents.

The people who read the papers and listen to all-sports radio talk shows and watch the highlight-film commercials come to the games expecting the fiction to be embodied. Their demands, and the speculations of the writers, take on a life of their own. Pretty soon the players may begin to notice a difference between what they do and what everyone out there *thinks* they do.

What Rivers is saying is that when the fans consume the media-packaged version of the NBA game, sometimes the players begin to consume it too. Some players are unable to resist completely the urge to become a little more like what people think they should be; it's a natural response, even a generous one.

"All of us want to give the fans a good time. All of us want to be liked, too. So if you keep reading all these stories about how you ought to be shooting more, or blocking more shots, or playing more of a power game because you *look* like a power forward, then you may feel a sort of obligation to try it. To give people what they want.

Look, every single player is at least a little bit insecure. Some more than others. Most fans don't know this—they think, 'Look at Dominique Wilkins, he's got it all, he must feel *great* about himself all the time!' But Nique is very insecure. We all are, at one time or another; we're all motivated a lot by fear, even Michael Jordan. Michael is *full* of fear, that all of a sudden one day he won't be able to dominate anymore—or that he won't want to. I heard him say he is quitting right away then—he knows he won't be able to live with the change and the doubt."*

In the history of the NBA some players have shown themselves susceptible to this oblique manipulation by the public's imagination and desire. It is hard to know what makes for the steadfastness that enables some players to resist the cries for unnatural modification. This resistance is probably the only thing Wilt Chamberlain lacked: As the most physically gifted athlete ever to play the game, he could do anything the press and public demanded—and he did. One season he would score an astonishing amount (averaging more than fifty points a game in 1961–62), one season he would show that he could pass to other guys (he led the league in assists in 1967–68), and so on. But Chamberlain learned the hard way that you could not satisfy the people you were trying to answer. As soon as you mastered one persona, they wanted another. There was always some new talent the public could imagine for you to exemplify.

Doc Rivers has managed to grow smartly through a very fine basketball career without having his head turned by the theorists and well-meaning modifiers. The 1992–93 season was his tenth in the NBA; he feels he has about three more in him, and there is no doubt he will get his playing time until he decides to step away. He is the kind of player coaches want on the floor, even when he has lost a little quickness or touch. In eight years with the Atlanta Hawks, Rivers quickly showed he could be depended upon to bring

* Doc told me this in July 1993. Jordan confirmed it when he announced his retirement three months later.

to each game several fundamental qualities: good ball-handling, great defense, just enough offensive dash to be dangerous when the chance arose, and the court smarts to take advantage of every opportunity that opened up for him or his teammates. Dependability made him a leader, for teammates as well as coaches. He is one of those rare basketball men who are equally revered by both the troops and the brass.

Except for losing, nothing shakes him. He is not sure how he became so resolute: "It wasn't really confidence. It was more like determination, though my mother would call it pure stubbornness. I always felt I knew best what I should do. Sometimes I knew what I should do was *listen,* to a good coach for instance. But I wouldn't listen to just anybody. My game was *my* game."

Also, Rivers says, he has never really had a "style" of play: "I wasn't good enough to stick to one great, original style." This protects him from the usual critiques. The player with a well-defined role or style, who always seems to play one way, is perhaps vulnerable to demands that he shift to another way. But a versatile player who cannot be pinned down is harder to fit into a fantasy.

"I have always come to the game ready to figure out what I needed to do to win on that particular night," Rivers says. "Whatever it takes, I'll do it. I'm a simple player—no flair. That makes it easier for me to adapt myself to the team's needs at the moment. Basketball is a game of rhythm—each stretch of a game has its own rhythm, and if you are trying to run to your *own* rhythm, you may not hear the one the *game* is running on. You have to keep yourself open to perceive the feeling that can arise between your teammates, that can suddenly turn a game around." He thinks. "It is intense. I love that. I have to be intense, myself—it's my key."

Rivers mentions a moment near the end of Game Five against the Hornets in last year's conference semifinal play-off series. "It was late in the game, it was very close, and we could all feel that for some minutes the game had been up for grabs. But neither team had snatched it. No one seemed to want to step up and take over. It was a *very* delicate sort of moment, everything was hanging there. Coach Riley called a time-out. One of our coaches, Dick Harter, said to me, 'Doc—somebody's got to *do* something.' So we went back out and I knew it was time to break Charlotte's back and I was going to start it. I made three steals, bang bang bang: took the ball out of Larry Johnson's hands, stole it from Dell Curry, tied up Alonzo Mourning for a jump ball. We lost the jump ball, actually, but it didn't matter: all of a sudden the whole team had the feeling, and we sent it right through Charlotte: *It's over, fellas.* And it was. They knew it. There was nothing they could do."

He smiles; it was a good victory against a team that didn't know how dangerous it really was, and the Knicks were relieved to get the Hornets out of town. After a moment to savor it, Rivers returns to the point. "I want to make sure it's clear that it wasn't just me who did this: I was just responding to the feeling, to the need of the team at that time. And I could perceive the feeling because I was ready to do anything. If we had needed a three right then, I would have tried to become a shooter of threes."

This story reflects the kind of year Rivers had in his first season with the Knicks. He filled many different roles, adjusting as the team met different challenges, suffered injuries, endured scoring slumps, faced hot teams or players. At one time or another he was: the starting point guard who would initiate the pressure on the opponent's defense; the level-headed fourth-quarter substitute who would settle down the frazzled play and refocus everyone on the fundamentals; the sudden-danger three-point gunslinger; the stop-dead defensive specialist; the fiery spirit unafraid to fight; the cool head keeping peace; the demure veteran stepping gracefully aside for the brash, talented youth in the Knicks' guard corps; the aggressive competitor beating the kids out for playing time . . .

"Everyone wants to be known for consistency," he says. "But consistency doesn't necessarily mean you do the same thing every night. You don't guard the same guy every night, do you? Your teammates are not equally hot or cold every night. You don't *feel* the same every night. What you want to be is consistent at figuring out what will work right *now*, for the *team*. The only consistency that matters is a string of W's. Anybody on the Knicks would gladly take up-and-down personal stats if he could get win after win."

Rivers mentions other players in the league who are adaptables rather than stylists. "Horace Grant. Magic Johnson—look how he switched to center for the final game of the championship series as a rookie, when Kareem was hurt. Michael Jordan. Everybody thinks of him as a shooter, but believe it or not, Jordan is probably the best player ever at adapting his own play to the needs of the team at the time. He changes his game *nightly*. There were six games in our play-off series against the Bulls, and Jordan was six different players. He's the greatest role player ever, and he can play all the roles."

Rivers wanted to be able to play them all too, even when he was a high-scoring high-school all-star in the basketball-crazy city of Chicago. A 1978 interview shows the sixteen-year-old sophomore eloquently defending his taste for making good passes instead of jacking up his scoring stats, as many fans were demanding. "Why should I shoot when a teammate has a better shot?" he said. "Just because people want to see me score more doesn't mean I should forget the game. A good pass is as hard to make as a good shot."

Perhaps the key part of this quote is the clear emphasis on the team instead of himself. If anything marks all of Rivers's talk about basketball, it is his devotion to the game's principle that five guys are better than one. Saying "Oh, I was just trying to help the team" has become the most automatically recited cliché in interviews. But with the best athletes, it is usually true. Certainly Rivers could not manufacture his constant excitement about being a part of something bigger than himself: He is always referring to teammates, their opinions about things, their stories, their families, their foibles, their talent or potential . . . To be with Doc Rivers for a day is to feel that there are always eleven other guys hanging in the background. The team is a constant presence. His joy in it is not merely an expression of selfless generosity; Rivers simply understands that the game he loves so much is entirely a matter of sharing.

"That's the reality of basketball: It's more than any one player and any one play, *always*," he says. "That's what makes something like the isolation of John's dunk so disruptive to a guy who knows his job. Or the attention I got after Game Four against Indiana last year, when I got hot and hit five threes and suddenly I was Mr. Downtown. I couldn't *wait* to start the next game and wipe my 'big moment' out of everybody's memory, including my own. I wanted to stay concentrated, and all that flurry of stuff breaks your concentration on what *really* matters, the *only* thing that really matters: how hard you work on the court. That's my worry about John's sudden stardom—that it will make it hard for him to keep his eye on the court. We need him. He is a tremendous player. He knows what he has to do, but with everybody whispering in your ear, it gets hard to focus."

Rivers says the only thing that helps you keep your equilibrium, that keeps you aware of the *real* game, is experience. "The focus on one moment like that, one guy—it just goes against everything we all know so well. It can kind of shake you out of what you know, if you aren't careful or experienced. Michael Jordan, for example, *has* the experience—he has handled the most incredible individual attention you can imagine, but he kept his eye on the right prize: the team championship. That takes a lot of commitment, but a lot of experience at deflecting things too."

He smiles. "But we all have to learn. I learned, and so has John. When this season starts, he will be The Man for a while. Everybody will be wanting a piece of him. Just watch, though. He'll handle it better this time around. He's an incredible player, and he's going to enjoy more than ever being on an incredible team."

His smile broadens. "I'll be there too. Hey, I can't wait for the *real* game to start."

The Uncle Plays

*B*asketball is not the real world," Doc has said. "The real world is the family."

Rivers means a few things more interesting and complex than these two simple statements seem at first to imply. Taken at face value, "The real world is the family" might be the slogan for a poster illustrating the '90s Theme, the way "Today is the first day of the rest of your life" summarized all the fresh-start attitudes of the '70s. "Family" is certainly the buzzword of any person or group wanting to demonstrate a heart—and a head—in the right place these days. Everything wicked in our culture, from street violence to low SATs, is attributed to breakdowns in this grand institution, which we speak of as one universal unit of harmonious nurture: The Family.

But Rivers is simply expressing the truth that *his* family— from the uncle who became an NBA player when Doc was a kid, to his parents, to his kids—has always defined for him what is generally referred to as reality: responsibilities, illusion-free choices, flattery-free critiques of one's actions.

As for basketball *not* being the real world, Rivers means, among other things, that NBA players have lived special lives of ease. Yes, it is hard to run, travel, and perform under public pressure as much as they do. But it is even more difficult to do many of the things they are usually *excused* from doing, things the nonathletes around them must come to grips with in school, college, adulthood: learn French or calculus, keep track of money, do laundry, earn affection from people, research and negotiate business relationships, find a job . . .

"From the moment a kid shows superior athletic talent, he is going to be taken care of," Rivers says. "The person who simply accepts it all along, who never stops and realizes he is getting an artificial, smooth ride, is probably not going to grow up quite right. It is possible for him to cruise through to his mid-thirties and believe he can do no wrong as a human being. No one has ever *made* him do anything unpleasant, whether it's passing a physics test or having to go out and find some friendly people to meet because he is lonely. The physics teacher isn't going to let you flunk. There are *plenty* of people waiting around to be your buddy the second you look up. Money is always there if you need it; you don't even have to ask."

So, Rivers explains, you've got young men who are larger than everybody else and richer than everybody else and more pampered than everybody else, whose biggest crisis—a shooting slump, reduced playing time—is completely contained by a game that has no real meaning relative to the challenges in the world. When there is a chance for interaction with such challenges, somebody else usually steps in to take care of the contact. If you mess up, someone usually cleans up. You can get away with a lot.

"But in your family," Rivers says, "you usually can't get away with *anything*. You do things most of the time on the basis of your feelings of responsibility for the people you love, feelings that are not really things you have any choice about. Your parents, your wife, your kids—you have the feelings, and the feelings make you aware of your responsibilities. When you get sly or lazy, people know you well enough to keep you honest. If you get to feeling like a big shot because you score thirty points one night, it won't cut you any slack with your kids when you break a promise to go get ice cream the next afternoon. They're not going to say, 'It's okay, Daddy, because you're such a star.' Forget it. You promise ice cream, you better deliver ice cream. Scoring thirty the night before doesn't even come into it."

Rivers says, "If you have been pampered by everybody else, your family is going to teach you to be a man by demanding things from you that you must be a man to give. I had to learn this as a husband first, then as a father. It was a tough lesson, but essential."

And of course your family is going to give just as much to you—as a man, not as a star athlete, Rivers explains. If you score three points instead of thirty, and your man has a triple double, and you clang a jumper off the rim at the buzzer in a two-point loss, it makes no difference to your kids. You are not a failure. You are a father. The hurt of a slump is still there, albeit diluted; but forcing yourself to put it away so you can be with your family can actually help you to get over it.

"I was explaining this to Hubert Davis after practice once," says Rivers. "Hubert was just out of college. He was up here in New York by himself. He is a great guy, and his enthusiasm for everything about basketball last season was very good for the team. But he was telling me that when he makes a mistake in a game, he lies awake for nights fretting about it, going over the play again and again in his head, wishing he could change it, psyching himself up for the next chance, all that sort of thing. He asked me what I did when I messed up in a game. How I handled the guilt and regret and frustration. I said, 'Hubert, I go home and there are a three-year-old and a five-year-old asleep with my wife in my bed, just waiting for me, and I climb into all that love and the game is *over*.' I knew it was impossible to communicate to him what the security of a family means. What it means, knowing that you will always be regarded as a good man by your family, when you may doubt that you were a good point guard for three particular minutes of a particular fourth quarter. He listened. His eyes were kind of far away. I thought he didn't understand, it was over his head, and he was just nodding to be polite while the old man rambled." Rivers laughs. "A week later he comes up to me after practice with this determined look on his face, and he says, 'You're right.' I had no idea what he was talking about. What was I right about? We hadn't spoken for days. He said, 'I've been thinking about the things you said about having a family. They make sense. I'm sure you're right.' I was impressed; it was clear he had been going over it all week."

For Rivers, not only does "real life" begin and end with the family, basketball began with the family too. Doc has an uncle named Jim Brewer, who preceded him by ten years as a hoops star at Proviso East High School (and later in the NBA as well). One night when Doc was in kindergarten, his parents took him to see his uncle play. It was the single most stunning experience in Doc's life.

"I didn't move for the entire game," he said. "I didn't go to the bathroom, go get a Coke, anything. I didn't talk, either. I watched. The whole thing completely captured me. It took me over. I understood what was going on in the game right away, and I didn't want to miss anything. It's still weird to me, to think of how strong the impact was. I remember that game. I remember almost the whole thing. It was *serious*."

Rivers says his mother was amazed. She took him to the next game. It too was serious. Pretty soon he was going to every game, sitting still through the entire contest, following every play with ferocious concentration.

"At first no one could believe it," he says. "I was a borderline hyperactive kid. I couldn't sit still or shut up, ever. Always into stuff, mischief, trouble. But at Papa's games (we called him Papa) I froze. I went to the games with an older white couple named Jacobs, who were devoted fans and never missed one. They understood what it meant to me, and they respected it. But other people would see me and think it was cute, a six-year-old paying such attention, or pretending to be so interested. But I wasn't being cute. And I certainly wasn't pretending. I was *studying*. This game was incredibly important to me."

Brewer's basketball games became important enough that they offered Doc's parents a point of leverage when the boy started to run with a bad crowd a few years later and got into trouble. When he was particularly bad, they warned him that he would be kept home from the next game if he didn't straighten up. He didn't. They kept him home.

"I was shocked," he says. "I don't think I believed they would do it. We all knew how much I counted on those games. At least we all thought we knew—but when they put me in my room and got ready to go themselves, I think we were all surprised at how desperate and miserable I was. Man, I never felt so lost. I wasn't so much mad, because I knew it was my fault, but I was frantic. I just could *not* miss the game! It was real hysteria." He smiles and rolls his eyes; the memory still makes him shake. "My parents were pretty shocked too, to see how effective a punishment it was. Listen, my dad was a *cop*—he wasn't exactly soft about discipline— but when he and my mom heard me wailing and pleading, they almost turned around on their way to the car and let me come. Almost. But they didn't. And I'll tell you what: That evening was the start of my turning away from messing with trouble."

As in all towns and cities and neighborhoods and streets, bad behavior with bad company was always an option. Boys learn pretty quickly which of the kids around them are likely to perform at which degree of badness—which kids play with trouble on the near side of the edge, and which play on the far. Rivers was experimenting with the thrills of both. Missing the Proviso East game in second grade was a restraint, he says; it kept him just a wee bit cautious and skeptical.

"I still wasn't a very good boy," he says. "My brother was always having to come after school with a note from my parents to pick me up because I had done some wild thing. Part of the problem was that I thought I wasn't as smart as other kids. I was getting okay grades, but I could tell other kids were learning things I was not. I didn't know this was because they were *studying* and I was not; I took the grades as a sign that I was doing what was necessary. This feeling of being dumb lasted until the eighth grade, when I had to take what is called the Constitution test. You had to pass this to be allowed to go to Proviso East High School, and I wanted to go there—because that was the place with the basketball tradition. So I decided to study for this test. It was the hardest thing in my life to do, because I didn't know *how* to study. But I did anyway. I worked to prepare for that test, thinking all the time that I was stupid but feeling like I had to do whatever I could, for the sake of basketball. Then I took it—and I got the second-best score in the entire school! Second best! Hey, I wasn't dumb after all! I just had to work, that's all; just like I had to work with b-ball."

He shakes his head. "Eighth grade was a little late to discover this, though. I missed a lot of basics; I am still trying to catch up. I wish I could tell every kid: What you skip will come back and haunt you, and it is a lot harder to make it up later. Do it *now*, do the work *now*, never mind how 'lucky' you feel because you get a soft teacher who lets you get by without studying or even being good. Somebody probably tried to tell me this, but I didn't listen. I felt just *fine* missing those basic lessons. And while I was missing them, I was acting *bad*.

"I don't really think I'm a case where, you know, a sport 'saved' me from some kind of 'life of crime.' It was never that dramatic," he says. "I was just kind of messing around, and we were all pretty young. I knew right from wrong and I had an excellent upbringing. I had an older brother who was street smart and tough and who didn't want me to *ever* get into trouble. I knew all these things too. They gave me a feeling of, you know, 'I'm not really bad, so I'll just *act* bad a little, or I'll just *do* this thing or that, because I know I'm not the kind of kid who is deep trouble.' "

He shakes his head and gives a mock shudder. "But now I recognize something. That's how a lot of kids get into real trouble. A lot of *good* kids. You don't have to be evil and out of control to ruin your life by doing something, just *one thing*, that is truly bad. In a way it's more dangerous when kids who are basically good mess around with stealing, or breaking something, or beating somebody up, or cheating, or doing the wrong kind of favor for the wrong kind of person, because these kids think they're not actually involved in evil. Being basically good gives you the illusion you are immune, your act won't have consequences. You're not *like* Freddy over there, who is completely nuts; you're just kind of *with* Freddy. Well—what scares me now is that I know being *with* is pretty much the same as being *like*. Doesn't matter what you know about right and wrong in the back of your mind; back of the mind never brought back somebody got killed by Freddy and the Good Boys, and no judge ever let somebody off because they had a nice upbringing, either. It's not what you know. It's what you do."

What Glenn Rivers started to do, in addition to separating himself from bad stuff, was play hoops. All day, every day. His home wasn't far from a park with outdoor courts, and he spent every hour he could shooting around. "In the summer or on weekends, when there wasn't school, I was gone before breakfast," he says. "My mom would come downstairs and I'd be gone. I didn't come home for lunch. Most of the time I missed dinner, too. The amazing thing is, she didn't make me give any of it up. She saw how good it was for me. She and my father knew where I was, and they told me: Just let us know where you'll be in case we want to check and make sure you're okay. The main court where I played was across the park from my grandmother's house, and I would see her sitting out on her porch, tiny and far away. But she could see me. I'm sure my parents drove by now and then too, just to see where I was. It was great. I was free. With my freedom I wanted to do nothing but play ball. There was no question of taking advantage of my parents' trust. I knew I was lucky. I just played."

He wasn't much good at first, of course, even when he was all alone. He couldn't really dribble or shoot. When he did play in a game, one-on-one or three-on-three, the man he was supposed to cover slaughtered him. But he was patient; he had to be. He was lucky enough to realize he was at the beginning of a long education. There was nothing else he could do but keep playing.

"Being aware that I was a beginner was important," he says. "It kept me from getting too humiliated. It kept me from getting too discouraged. It kept me from taking shortcuts. A kid who is in too much of a hurry will get so he can make one particular shot pretty well and then that's all he will ever try to take in games. But basketball involves so many different kinds of skills, and the only way you get into them is by trying to do them when you can't. I guess I stumbled onto the right attitude: I wanted to be good as fast as I could, but I wanted to take enough time so that I was *really* good. I just loved playing, and seeing little signs of progress. So it didn't bother me as much if I was the worst player on the court. It bothered me, but not so that I forgot my progress. I'd be pretty bad in a game, and my man would be talking all over me, 'You suck, I'm killing you, ya ya ya,' but I might be thinking, 'Hey, I switched the dribble to my left hand and drove pretty well before he blocked my shot. I couldn't do that yesterday. I'm getting better.' "

As he got better, Rivers began to play on Boys' Club and school teams, where coaches complemented his private education with a different sort of instruction. "I taught myself many of the individual fundamentals," he says, "but this is a team game, and all you are really doing when you shoot alone for hours is getting ready to hit that shot as part of a team. It can be a team that is put together for one game on one day on a playground, or it can be a team that practices together every day and plays a whole schedule. It's a perfect balance, if you are lucky. You spend all that time alone, dribbling and cutting and shooting, talking to yourself, pretending you're playing an opponent, pretending you have teammates, pretending the fans are watching every move, pretending the radio announcer is narrating what you do . . . and then one day you *do* have teammates, and opponents, and maybe even fans and an announcer. It's private plus public, alone plus together, freedom plus responsibility."

Rivers was fortunate to find himself in the tutelage of *good* coaches. Perhaps they recognized his tendency to play the game in its wholeness, or perhaps they inspired him to do so. In any case, they were teachers of the entirety of basketball, and he took to their lessons well.

"When I was in elementary school, we used to have practices in which the offense had to score a basket, starting under the other basket, against *eight* defenders, but the offense *could not dribble*. Against eight defenders. Move the ball all the way upcourt, work a play, get a good shot, a rebound, set another play—all without putting the ball on the floor. This is a sophisticated drill for teaching ball movement, and teaching how to move without the ball to get open— and this is *elementary* school." He mentions early defensive drills, workouts on rebounding, pick plays—all of them oriented toward team play.

"Coaches have a challenge when they get a bunch of kids without much talent and a couple who are much farther along," he says. "How do you bring the mediocre or inexperienced players up without holding the hotshots down? How do you avoid just depending on your stars in games and letting the others sit around and watch them go? All the way to the NBA, this is a problem for coaches, because even in college there is a big gap on a team between the best players and the rest. In the NBA everybody is pretty great, though not everyone performs as the big scorer. There is less of a gap between the top guy and the twelfth. Even so, sometimes any team can sit back and watch while Mr. Startime takes over, and usually that hurts the whole team's game. For coaches with beginners, this is a big challenge."

Rivers feels he has had great luck with coaches: He got the right coach at the right time, and moved along in his understanding and development of team play. At the same time, most of his hours were spent on the playground, where his individual gifts emerged under a different sort of pressure.

"After a while, instead of spending so much time playing by myself, I was going to the playgrounds where the good games were. One day it would be one place, in a certain neighborhood; all the players would be there, waiting their turns to play. On another day, everybody would be somewhere else. You'd hear where the games were, and try to get there." He explains the general outline of playground rules. A game is going on, full court, five-on-five. One team wins, and they get to remain on the court to play the next challenger. The losers go to the back of the line. Generally it is not a whole team but a single kid who is waiting for his turn to pick a team to challenge the winners.

"Everybody wanted to play. Sometimes you'd wait three hours just to get one game. For a long time I was one of the youngest and worst players, so when it was my turn to pick a team and play, some of the better guys would try to push me aside. 'You ain't playing, get outta here, this is *my* game,' like that. My brother was always there, and he would step up and point at me and say, 'This is *his* game, *he* waited, *he* is going to play.' Nobody messed with my brother. So the guys who had been trying to run me over would suddenly be my buddies, bending down and smiling in my face and saying, 'Hey, my man, can I run with you? Come on, we'll beat these scrubs, yo, my man, little man, let me get a run . . .' I'd always say, 'Let's wait and see who loses.' I was smart enough to know I wanted the best players as teammates, and if some players on the losing team in the current game were better than the guys begging me on the side-lines, I was going to pick the better guys. Because I wanted to win: Winning meant you got to keep playing.

"So I would pick my team and we'd play. I would be the last man anyone wanted to pass to. So I'd find plenty to do without the ball—play defense, try to box a guy out, make steals, run around like crazy and get so open my teammates *had* to pass to me. Little by little I would get my hands on the ball. And I got better and better."

Rivers says those years of being the youngest and worst contributed more than anything in his basketball life toward making him good.

"The best advice I can give any kid who wants to become a good ballplayer is this: Play as much as you can with people better than you are. Preferably older and bigger, too. It can be very frustrating, but it's a great challenge. You have nothing to lose—if you do well against them, you have *really* done something, but if you don't match them early on, you can't feel like a complete failure, because after all they are ahead of you. This isn't an excuse, though—when you are on the court you have to forget they are better and pretend it is natural for you to beat them. Then there is the education: When you play with better players, you get to learn from their game. A guy keeps beating you with a crossover move, so you begin to practice it yourself. You have witnessed it firsthand enough, you know how it worked against *you,* so you can master it. It's like going to school. Better players give you a fantastic opportunity. The trade-off is, you don't get the chance to feel like the big star of the game very much." He smiles. "But just wait. I can promise you: Your day will come."

Patrick

*P*atrick Ewing is a lot like Moses Malone was to me. I heard so much about both of them before I got to know them. When I played against Patrick, I had the impression he was one mean, unhappy man. And because Patrick—like Moses—doesn't play the media game, the smile-and-make-a-good-impression game, I had this idea that he was one of those guys who just wants to do his job, doesn't want to lead, wants to be left alone. So when I came to the Knicks, I was in for a big shock. Patrick isn't anything like what people think. He is one of those players the media have completely missed. He is a very nice guy, a very smart guy, a very thoughtful guy, and the best leader there is. An incredible leader. His will carried *everybody* at various points last year. We all knew we could lean on Patrick a little; but more important, we all knew we had *better* play. Patrick does that—he makes a guy think, 'I better work, because *he's* working, and he's watching, too, and I don't want him mad at me.'

"Even before I played with Patrick, whenever people asked who I would draft among all the centers in the NBA, I always said Patrick. The main reason is that he is just so intimidating, so fearsome. The effects of his defense don't show up in the stats. It's yet another case of statistics failing to reveal the real game. People will flip through their stat sheets and say, 'Ewing's blocks are way down this year. He's losing his defensive skills.' What they don't know is that maybe Patrick's blocks are down because he's getting *better* at blocking shots. So people are not even *trying* those shots anymore.

"The number of shots Patrick alters is *huge,* but most of them never even get attempted. A guard makes a move past me and heads for the lane, but when he gets to the foul line, he sees Patrick ahead, glaring and all set to eat his shot. So instead of beating me and going in for a layup and getting the layup blocked, the guy stops, thinks, 'What do I want to do?' and I catch up to him. Or he passes off to somebody in the corner, who now has to take a twenty-footer.

"It is very hard for writers to know what players are thinking. But on the court *we* know, we know what shot a guy was going to take and we can see when he changes his mind. And Patrick is the best defensive player in the league *in the heads of his opponents.*

"As for offense—well, I hope Patrick will soon get the recognition he deserves for being the best-shooting big man in the history of the game. The *best.* His jump shot is an outrageous weapon—it destroys teams. They get the defense all set, they play Patrick well down low and don't let us get the ball into the post, we are whipping it around the perimeter and the twenty-four is down to five–four–three—then Patrick steps out and grabs the ball and hits a twenty-five-footer. *Skoosh!* Man, that demoralizes people. He is an amazing shooter, through talent, but through willful hard work, too. He decided he needed that shot, so he made it. There has *never* been a big man who could shoot that shot as well as Patrick. Never. People say, 'What about Cowens? What about McAdoo?' Well, they were great shooters—but they were only six nine; they were power forwards playing out of position. Patrick Ewing is a legitimate, bona fide *big man,* seven feet tall, a classic center. And he can shoot the prettiest, meanest jump shot there is.

"Another thing I like about Patrick: He doesn't have a stop button. He goes hard all the time. He played so hard in *every* practice and *every* game last year that his knees were absolutely killing him by the play-offs. But he will never slow down. He has a will that cannot be slowed down, and for Patrick that will leads directly to *work*.

"It's funny—the best players I have played with and against, as I look back, are the hardest workers. Magic. Bird. Moses. Sidney Moncrief. Patrick Ewing. Those are some hard, hard-working guys. They all have this in common. And they're all great. It's not a coincidence, is it?"

Do It

W hen I was a kid," says Doc Rivers, "I got to know the great Austin Carr. He played with my uncle Jim Brewer for the Cleveland Cavaliers. He was a tremendous ballplayer, a great scorer—his last two years at Notre Dame he averaged thirty-eight points, and he did very well in the NBA, too. My youngest son is named for him.

"One time I decided to ask him to teach me the tricks of the trade. So I came up with all of these specific things I wanted to learn about different parts of the game: how to get better at dribbling, how to jump higher, how to improve this shot and that shot.

"And he gave me an answer I thought wasn't even an answer. I thought he was joking. He said, 'Want to learn how to dribble? Dribble. You want to jump higher? Jump. Want to figure out how to shoot? Shoot.' I said, 'Hey! Why don't you tell me something!' He said, 'I'm telling you the truth. What you want to learn, *do*. Practice it over and over. It will improve.' "

Rivers seems always to think about the frustrations of beginners, emphasizing the need to accept being bad at the start, the need to take time to improve, the need to measure success against better players, etc. This emphasis emerges largely because he recognizes that even a seasoned ballplayer is essentially a beginner all over again when he wants to acquire a new move, a new shot, a new defensive technique. Frequently Doc describes his own frustrations, on days when his left-handed dribble needs work, or his long jumper won't fly right—and he sounds just like a nine-year-old who can't quite figure out how to hit a running layup.

"The easiest time to quit is at the beginning," he says. "Not just because of frustration. Most people don't quit because they aren't good—they quit because they are bored, bored by the endless repetition of practicing a skill or a move or a shot. It is incredibly tedious. You do it over, and over, and over. And then over some more. It takes a long time in this game. But you just have to keep doing things forever. All the lessons and tips in the world won't help you unless you practice them relentlessly. Knowledge becomes action only by endless practice. Watching films, weight training, all that stuff helps, but only if you make it part of your game by doing it enough.

"Austin Carr told me to use the great sprinter of the time, Bob Hayes, as an example. Now I use Carl Lewis. If Carl Lewis wants to work on his speed, he gets a guy to time him and he goes out and runs a hundred meters *as fast as he can*. Then he spends the rest of the day running hundreds to try to beat that time. If he doesn't beat it, next day he comes out and runs until he does. Then there you are: He has increased his speed. Not by doing weird drills and lifting leg weights and taking his stride apart on the videotape, but by *running as fast as he can*. Videos are fine, but speed is real.

"It's the same with basketball. For example, if you want to jump higher, take a piece of tape in the tips of your fingers and stand next to a wall and jump as high as you can, and stretch your hand as high as you can stretch, and slap that tape against the wall. Then spend an hour trying to touch a spot on the wall above that tape. It may take you a month, but you will get higher just by trying to jump higher. You will teach your legs to *do* it. Then you move the tape up and keep going. Practice by doing, do by practicing."

Rivers says basketball camps are good, but adds that "a camp is not going to increase your scoring average next season by two points a game, or cut your turnovers by two a game, or increase your steals or rebounds by two a game. Just coming to camp and learning *how* to do these things does nothing. You have to work with what you learn. Work on a skill in practice, and then, when you are getting confident about it, integrate it into your games. If it doesn't work, over and over in games, don't damage your confidence or your team by persisting with it. That's a waste of energy. Save it for practice *after* the games. One day you'll bring it back into play and it will work fine."

He shrugs. "I keep saying this, but I'll say it again: No matter what age you are, or what level, there are always things you wish you could do. Every year I have to do what I just described. I find some aspect of my game I wish I could execute better, and I discover it isn't coming together during games. So I 'retire' that little part from active duty. I leave it out of the games. But every day I practice it, over and over, that one thing—say it's finishing my drives to the left with a layup instead of pulling up for a jumper. Eventually I get it down. And you know what I do then?"

Rivers grins. "I *save* it. Especially if the play-offs are coming up. Because before the play-off series starts, the other team will put my game *as I have been playing it recently* through all kinds of analysis. The coaches will show films and say, 'Now, we notice this year Rivers always pulls up and shoots when he goes to his left—he doesn't drive all the way to the hole anymore from the left dribble. From the right he likes to go all the way in, but not left. So if he starts left, guys, count on the jump shot.' The man guarding me listens to his coaches. He's all set for that jumper, and when I move left he is ready to stop and jump, just waiting for the moment . . . and I blow by him. I am going to *kill* him in that series, because I have developed the secret weapon."

He laughs, but holds up an admonitory finger. "It's fun when it works. Say I make the surprise move late in a game and put us up two and we win. That's *fun*. But the hours and hours that lead up to that, all that left-hand dribbling and the layups, that was definitely *not* fun. That was a drag. But you have to do it. You have to concentrate on doing exactly what you aren't good at, in practice. You want to go back to doing things you *are* good at, because that's more comfortable. But keep at the harder work. It will come. I promise."

He holds up ten fingers. "Remember, this is a simple game but a *hard* game. Look at me. Ten years as a pro, and I still have plenty of things I work on, things that frustrate me because I can*not* get them down on a certain day. I will practice something over and over and it isn't happening, and I go home thinking, 'Man! I am *never* going to get this.' But eventually I do. It is unbelievable how long it can take, and how suddenly it can come. It is also unbelievable how good it can feel when you've got it."

Chris Mullin

The biggest difference between college ball and the NBA is the fact that in college you faced a really great player, an All-American, about once every six or seven games," says Doc. "You'd play a team that had one terrific guy every now and then; otherwise you'd face solid college-level guys. If you were a great player yourself, this means you were almost always being guarded by lesser players, ordinary players. You could blow them all away, just play full-tilt the whole time. You could play in only one gear: high gear. That was quicker and stronger than everybody else.

"In the NBA, every single game is against a team with *five* All-Americans on the floor. Every player in the league is pretty much as good as you are. Everybody is as quick, as strong, as determined, as mean, as gifted . . . so you simply do not blow these people away the way you did the fellows in your conference in school. I watch as it hits every rookie: 'Geez, I'm going as fast as I can, and these guys are all keeping up with me!'

"I would like to tell every rookie to sit back and watch Chris Mullin play for a couple of games. Chris Mullin is the King of Tempo. He is not fast, but he knows the great secret: A defensive man will have to adjust to your pace. If you slow down, he slows down too. Once both of you are going slow, if you can suddenly increase your speed at the right moment, you catch him by surprise and blow by him. It doesn't matter whether that new speed is actually very fast or not. What matters is that relative to the pace you established, it is fast *enough*. It is a relativity thing. If you play for a while in second gear, then shifting up to third makes you look pretty quick.

"Chris Mullin has more gears—more well-paced speeds—than anybody, and he is a master at using them. A defender has a terrible time adjusting. After playing Chris, his man will walk off the court talking to himself: 'I am faster than that dude, I am stronger than that dude, I am bigger than that dude, but he ate my lunch! He scored thirty-two on me! How did he do it?' Mullin knows how he did it, believe me. And he can do it on almost anybody, because when you set the pace, you are in charge of speed."

Loving It

*T*he great thing about defense is that you cannot let up for a second," Doc Rivers says. "It requires complete commitment, complete concentration. I remember one play-off game between Atlanta and Milwaukee. I was guarding Sidney Moncrief, a great offensive player, and for some reason I was having a terrific defensive game against him. Usually he did pretty well against me, but this game I was frustrating him every time up the court. Just one of those games where everything I tried worked."

He smiles ruefully. "Well, there we were, with a pretty good lead, and it was the fourth quarter, and somebody on their team took a shot and for some reason I didn't block Sidney out. I don't know why—didn't know why at the time—but I just didn't keep the intensity for that *one* split second, did not finish that *one* duty. And he was by me in a flash and tip-dunked the ball. *Koosh!* I was kicking myself—*you idiot, you had him and you let him back in the game!* Because the cat was out of the bag now. Sidney woke up and played great down the stretch, but fortunately we won anyway. I almost blew it for us, just because I relaxed for an instant."

Rivers says there are a lot of players you can psych out early in the game, players who will go into a hole if you stop them three or four times. They lose their confidence, they start to doubt and think and second-guess, they sulk. "But you can't just put them down and count on them to stay there," he says. "You have to keep the pressure on. An NBA player, given a chance, will pull himself out of a sulk in a hurry. A great shooter who is getting killed by a defender will probably keep shooting anyway, looking for the touch to return, and if you let up a little and he makes a couple, then he's back, and he's feeling even better than ever, and he's going to kill *you* now.

"The most terrible thing in the world is to work hard to get a guy down, to spend the whole first quarter and half the second making sure you frustrate him at everything he tries, and at last you've got him down and you know you can keep him there, but the coach decides to give you a rest. He puts in a guy for you, and he doesn't keep the pressure on your man. Maybe he doesn't know what you were doing, maybe his style or skills aren't as good a match for the man you had down. But in any case, it's not the same, and your man senses it. He senses there's an opening, and he takes advantage of it, pops up off the bottom, makes a couple of shots, and next thing you know he's *back*! Just in time for you to go back in." Rivers growls. "Of course, you can't just put him down again now. He's got the feeling back. So the rest of the game it's *you* who are scrambling." He sighs. "After the game, the coach says, 'Hey, how come you let up on so-and-so?' All you can do is shake your head."

For the record, Rivers says Pat Riley is the best coach he has ever seen at sensing what each player is doing on the court at a particular time. "As far as I'm concerned, the coach's primary role in the NBA is to get the right people on the floor at the right time. Calling plays, teaching techniques, all that stuff isn't nearly as important as reading what's going on in all the matchups. If somebody is shooting hot, if somebody has a good defensive thing going, if somebody has got a lot of spring in his legs going for the boards, then you leave him in. If somebody is tired, or missing connections with teammates, or getting too angry, or just not feeling into what's happening on the floor at the moment, then you make a change. No player is ever going to admit he needs to come out of a game, so the coach has to make the move when he spots something. If the team's play gets better, the move was right. If the team's play falls apart, either you made the wrong move or you needed to make another move with it. There's nothing hidden out there. A coach gets to see it all. If the wrong guy is in the wrong spot at a key moment, then it's not just the player's fault if he doesn't get the job done. The coach needs to look ahead based on what he sees."

Rivers says the players respect a coach who reads the game well, because basically he is allowing them to run the game as long as they are succeeding. "Often the players go out with a game plan the coach has decided upon, but we discover something that works better. Maybe one of their guys is a little slow tonight and the man he's guarding feels quicker than usual, so we go to him. Maybe one of our players starts hitting shots out of his mind and we want to let him string it along as far as possible. Maybe we see one of their guards get a little panicky when we improvise a trap on him, so we start doing it more. There's always something that shows up, and if we find it and exploit it, Riley will let us roll. Some coaches will not—they'll call a time-out, remind us of the game plan, try to force us to play the coach's game. Not Riley. He recognizes that it's the players' game. We *love* that. Of course, when he pulls you out, you think he's crazy. Every player is trying to contribute, and we all believe we are helping. But a coach has to know that what matters is the overall net gain of the team while you are on the floor. You may hit four shots in three minutes, but if the team was ahead by six when you came in and it is now up only two despite your heroics, then you are coming out. Your play was not what the team needed. And if the play picks up, you have to give him credit. And he is very sensitive to the player's self-respect; he always lets the player know that he believes in the player's commitment to the team. Riley never accuses anyone of being selfish; some coaches do that first thing. Riley lets you know he believes you want to stay in the game because you feel your play benefits the *team*. He earns his credibility that way: by letting us do our work as long as it works, and by making the right moves in spite of what you may feel."

He thinks for a moment. "I don't mean to slight Riley as a ⌐egist, because he does plan plays and he does want the play ᴄᴏ ɪun. Every coach wants the play to run—that's the coach's job. But if you break the play, it's okay, even if you miss—as long as you tried something you were good at. As long as you stuck to one of your strengths. John Starks is the biggest play-breaker of all time, but Riley lets him try things because John makes things happen for us. John screws up defenses worse than his broken plays mess *us* up. If he tries to do something that's not his game, or if anyone does—if Pat Ewing starts putting up threes on the break—then Riley will come down on the innovator. He's fair. He wants you to do what you're good at, and he'll let you try it when you think the moment is right, whether he planned it or not."

Rivers says the Knicks last year were the best team he's seen at putting forth the sort of spontaneous generosity that allows players to discover unexpected felicities on offense. "Look, each of us is a man with great pride. Each of us believes he should take the big shots, especially if the basic plan is to run plays that way. But we all want the team to win, so if all of a sudden one guy gets hot, he'll keep getting the ball, all night if he keeps hitting. Anybody would prefer to see a teammate score a more certain basket than to take a less certain shot himself."

Doc's favorite times in a basketball game come when the called play gets broken, when either a defender doesn't do what he's expected to, or an offensive teammate gets tied up or misses a move. "That's when you get to find out what works," he says. "The pressure's on, you've got maybe eighteen seconds, you look around and catch a couple of quick glances, you see a defensive guy's feet stutter a little, you sense his man move, you spin and pass, and *skoosh!* Two!" He grins and raises a fist. "It gets so creative so fast. You rely on everything you know, everything you've ever learned about the game and all that, but really it's like you've never played before in a way. Everything feels new and fresh, and you feel like you are inventing the whole game with your teammates. Those are the best times. You can beat anybody when it's working like that. You don't want the game to stop. If the other coach calls a time-out, you go to the bench and your coach talks but you aren't listening. You're just trying to keep the rhythm going, to keep the feeling, to keep the communication open. Then you get back out on the floor and *whoosh,* you're off again, into it."

It is clear that for Rivers this spontaneous momentum is the heart of basketball. And as with all of the things he loves about the game, it is a matter of teamwork going beyond what individuals could possibly do on their own.

"Hey, what can I say? It's a team game." He laughs. "Look. When I'm through playing in two or three years, I want to coach. And then I want to be a general manager. I want to win the championship as a player, as a coach, and as a GM—that's my lifetime goal as far as basketball goes. And you can believe that the thing I will always be looking to create and preserve is this special teamwork thing. It's not something you can always predict by looking at stats or personalities or anything. You can make a trade you think will bring just the right guy into the club, the right personality, but he won't fit, he's just wrong in some way. You can go after a player with exactly the statistical achievements your team needs—you're weak in offensive rebounds so you get an offensive rebounder, you turn the ball over too much so you get a solid guard, whatever—but it turns out that competence in that weak area isn't enough. I know a few GM's and coaches very well, and they have a tough, tough time assembling the right group of players. All I can say is: When I am a coach, and later a GM, if I am lucky enough to get it right, I will recognize that I've got a team, and I'll do everything possible not to mess it up. Sometimes that's a coach's best move: to make *no* move. Sometimes the best trading decision for a GM is *not* to make any trades."

Rivers thinks for a minute about players. "I'll tell you what it all comes down to. The main guys you hope to get as teammates are those who love the game. Those are the ones who will *play*."

Those who . . . ? Does he mean there are players who do *not* love the game?

He looks amused at my naïveté in assuming pro basketball players are crazy about basketball; he also looks quite sad that I am wrong. "In the NBA there are a lot of kinds of people, so there are a lot of kinds of players. Just like in other professions. Some people take a job because it pays well, and they work with that incentive, and they try to excel with the goal of making more money and gaining more prestige, even though the work may not interest them all that much in itself. Some people take a job because they've just kind of been channeled that way for most of their lives. Some people go into a line of work because something inside them *makes* them do that work—they love it so much, they can't do anything else and be happy. We have all these kinds in the NBA."

He counts off on his fingers. "There are players who are pure professionals—meaning they are here to do a job. They play hard, give an excellent effort, try to win if possible, take their work seriously. But their hearts are not in it, especially. They are not, you know, *fulfilled* by a great quarter of basketball. They are not especially stirred by a tough win, in a deep way. Or a tough loss. Don't get me wrong—these guys are not uncommitted, they are not slack, they are not just going through the motions. They work hard for their good pay, the way a corporate guy works hard for his. But a lot of the time, like the corporate guy, they are just bored."

Bored? In the NBA? Fighting Alonzo Mourning for a rebound can be boring? Trying to scoop a layup under David Robinson, or block a Dan Majerle jumper? *Dull?*

Rivers laughs. "Well, I can guarantee you nobody who is bored is going to get anywhere *near* a rebound Alonzo wants, because Alonzo comes to play—you'd better care more about that rebound than anything in the world if you're going to take it away from *him*.

But, yeah—the guys I'm talking about have gotten bored with basketball. Some of them even *hate* the game. Especially the guys in the second group I mentioned, the people who were kind of brought along from sixth grade up to be nothing but pro basketball players. Because they were tall, most likely. A lot of these guys were forced to go out for the basketball team by coaches or parents, and nobody ever even asked them if they *wanted* to play basketball. Maybe they wanted to take piano lessons or something, you know? But they went along, and soon they noticed life was a lot easier, teachers were giving them good grades, girls liked them, their dads were happy with them, people knew them, gave them anything they wanted, colleges gave them scholarships and money, and pretty soon somebody offers them a couple million dollars a year just to keep on playing this stupid game. So they do. But they don't like it any more now than they did in sixth grade; in fact, by now they probably despise and resent it. They wake up every day and dread hearing a dribble. You can't blame them a bit."

Rivers shakes his head as if to clear it of such evil. "But then there are the guys who are here because they wouldn't want to be anywhere else in the world, *anywhere*." He relaxes and grins. It has pained him to talk about the bored and resentful players; now he's talking about *his* people. "These are the ones who fell in love with the game the way you fall in love with a person for life. They just can't get tired of it. They want to be around it all the time. They are devoted to it. When they put on their uniforms, it's like for the first time, every game, but it's the most familiar, comfortable thing in the world too. Once the game starts, they don't care if it lasts forever. You could tie them up in the parking lot and chain them to a car, and by halfway through the first quarter they'd come out on the floor dragging the car behind them, 'Hey, I'm open!' They have wanted all their lives to play basketball with the best players in the world and here they are, doing it, and they would do it all day every day if they could. They know for a fact they are the luckiest people in the world."

Do these players sometimes have a happy-just-to-be-here mentality? Are they so tickled to be guarding Scottie Pippen that they don't try that extra bit to stop every shot he takes? Is a loss a little thing compared to the magnitude of their fulfillment in the game itself? Are they less competitive than others?

"No. They are *more* competitive," Rivers says. "It's not even *close.*" He thinks for a minute. "Here's what it is. If you love a sport, there are two things that are included in the love you feel: one, to play just incredibly well, to be awesome at the game; and two, to win. There is never a time when the desire to be good and the desire to win are not a part of the whole feeling. I would say you cannot love basketball and feel indifferent about winning. You cannot love a game and not care right to the heart about winning, every time you play. It's just *there,* when you pick up the ball and face another guy. It's the challenge. It's what makes it fun, instead of just sort of an exercise of skill."

Rivers is known to be a gracious fellow but a ferocious competitor, too. He walks the line perfectly between being a jerk about victory at all costs and being a little too good-humored. He'll gripe about a foul call, but he won't moan so much that he falls into the obvious anger and self-pity that become distractions. He'll make a nice comment to a friendly opponent before the game, but he won't break his team's daunting enmity with a fond gesture during the battle. Frankly, if he had to choose one or the other, he'd rather you thought he was a mean jerk than a nice guy, on the court.

"You have to find the right kind of meanness," he says. "You don't have to hate anybody, exactly, but you have to hate to lose and then recognize that the other guys are trying to make you do so. For sure you cannot feel any kindness for them. For me, it's not necessary to psych myself up by exaggerating all these negative feelings about the people I'm playing against. That works for some guys, but it's not me. I just find my natural competitiveness excludes any softness toward the other team. The guys wearing the different uniforms, they're not my *colleagues* or something; they're my *oppo-*

nents. They are trying to take the thing I want: championship. I see them as thieves. I *want* that championship, and they're stealing from me." He thinks. "Maybe I *do* build a kind of hatred from that, for the court. But it's not the kind that poisons you. It inspires you."

Rivers says he cannot understand it when players act chummy toward opponents. "Saying 'Nice shot!' when a guy has scored on you? Give me a break! I'll tell you what—if a guy says 'Nice shot!' you know that's one guy you can beat whenever you want. I remember one time in Atlanta. Michael Jordan came down the lane and dunked over Jon Koncak. Nothing against Jon, but he's not exactly a killer. He *is* seven feet tall, though, and here Jordan humiliates him with a big, violent dunk right in his face. And Koncak turns to him with a sort of sheepish smile and holds out his hand for Jordan to slap, to give him five. Jordan looks at him, looks at his hand, with the single greatest expression of contempt I have ever seen, like 'What the *bleep* are you *doing,* man?' and he trots back upcourt shaking his head. I felt the same way: What the *bleep* are you *doing*?"

He goes on. "The worst person in the world you could show that kind of weakness to is Jordan. He's obviously got incredible skills, but I would say his best quality as a player is his competitiveness, his concentration on one thing: winning. Everything that happens on the court during a game he evaluates in terms of how it contributes to that overall goal, whether he can get an edge here, whether that is a weakness there, and so on. He zeroes in on any opening. If he catches you admiring him, you are dead."

When Rivers speaks of Jordan, it is plain he respects but does not especially admire him. As with most things he discusses, Rivers has the gift for seeing Jordan for what he is, acknowledging great stuff without having to go further emotionally, into adoration or resentment. Jordan is a great player, a winner, and that's that. So what? You can see that Rivers's habitual clarity and balance serve him well when it comes to MJ: Preserving a neutrality about the guy is probably difficult. Jordan is, of course, the main challenge facing every NBA player with aspirations for a championship, and the main challenge for any guard playing against the Bulls. Rivers accepts the challenge, and he has no reason to feel he's not up to it. Like any opponent, Jordan is there to be beaten.

Their rivalry goes way back, and though Rivers has played exceptionally well against Jordan and may have "won" a few of the battles, Doc cannot see it that way. Jordan has three championships, Rivers has none; therefore, for now Jordan is the only one who can claim any kind of victory. It's that simple, and there's no use griping, just as there's no use celebrating the partial "victory" of having held Michael below his average or fouling him out in this game or that. Rivers acknowledges all that Jordan has accomplished; if there is anything he respects most about Jordan, it is probably the fact that Jordan plainly felt he had done nothing—never mind the scoring titles and MVPs—until his team won the championship. That's Rivers's kind of values. Jordan's emphatic pursuit of the title was a respectable testimonial for the competitive team spirit: The superduper king of media, endorsements, idolatry, and individual achievements was so manifestly hungry for the team goal. Jordan, like Rivers, is one of those who love the game.

Rivers plays with the rivalry a bit in public—an autograph seeker wearing a Jordan T-shirt is told "What, are you kidding?" and laughs, and another well-wisher wearing *another* Jordan shirt has his compliment answered in kind: "Great season, Doc!" he says; Rivers replies, "Awful shirt, Mike!"

During the 1993 play-offs, the rivalry literally came home to Rivers in a comical but poignant way. His son Jeremiah, who was five at the time, was not really a basketball fan. But he knew Michael Jordan from all of Jordan's television commercials and T-shirts and general cultural presence, and he knew everybody was supposed to like Mike and want him to win. When the Knicks beat the Hornets and advanced to the Eastern Conference semifinals against the Bulls, Jeremiah let it be known that he was rooting for Michael Jordan.

"But that means you are rooting against Daddy," Kris Rivers explained.

"But I have to be for Michael Jordan," said Jeremiah.

"What about Daddy?"

"Well, I'm for Daddy, too."

"But only one of them can win, Jeremiah. They are both after the same prize, and there is only one prize."

Jeremiah could not bring himself to understand that he could not legitimately pull for Michael Jordan without wishing for his father to lose. *Kids are for Michael Jordan,* according to the programming. At one point he came to Doc with an idea: "Daddy, how about if you score more points than Michael Jordan, but his team wins the game?"

"Good idea, J-Man," said Rivers with a smile. "But how about if we switch it? Let Michael score more points. The Knicks will take the game."

Jeremiah's sister Callie, age three, had no problem, however. As Jeremiah worked out his agonizing dilemma, Callie would announce to him: "I'm for the *Knicks.*" Over and over, "I'm for the *Knicks.*" After the Bulls eliminated New York and went on to play the Suns in the finals, Jeremiah was free to resume the cultural imperative of pulling for MJ. But Callie was not fazed. Her mom carefully explained to her what had happened. "I understand," she said. "It's the Suns against the Bulls." Then Jeremiah said, "So *now* who are you for?"

"I," said Callie with a proud smile, "am for the *Knicks.*"

Mo

"Maurice Cheeks had great physical talent," Doc recalls, "but that was not the best thing about him. What I liked most in his game was his ability to do the critical thing at exactly the critical time.

"You could study the box score of every game Maurice ever played in and get no idea of what he had done in the game. Sure, sometimes he had flashy stats—twenty-two points shooting six-fifty from the floor, six steals, fifteen assists. He had plenty of nights like that. But there were nights when he scored only seven points and got two rebounds and made three assists, in forty-six minutes on the floor. Somebody who believes in stats—which I don't, I think stats are completely worthless and individual stats right after the game will not be allowed in my locker room when I coach—that stat person would say, 'Cheeks had an off night.'

"But Maurice *never* had an off night. What you could not understand unless you were there was that every single basket and rebound and pass came at a point in the game when the team needed just that play more than anything. Of his three baskets, one would be a layup off a steal with three seconds left in the first half just after the opponents had made a run and cut the 76ers' lead to five. *Boom*, Maurice sends them into the locker room down seven and thinking '*Damn*, we could have been within three!' and they kick themselves through halftime. His next basket would be a long jumper off a broken play with two seconds left on the shot clock, at a time when his team hadn't scored in four straight possessions and the opponents were really getting renewed confidence in their defense. Then, *skoosh!* Mo hits a three and the defense sags, muttering, '*Damn,* we were holding them!' His last two points would come on free throws with fifty seconds left and his team up only four.

"That's the way he played. I could almost say that Maurice Cheeks made nothing *but* big baskets, or big steals, or big passes. When a critical moment arose, he was there to do exactly the right thing. He had the intelligence and the guts to step up when his team needed him. That's the best you can say about any player. No one was ever better at it, in my experience. If I had to choose one player to shoot a free throw with no time left and the championship on the line, it would be Mo."

Fatherhood

My most important job right now is not playing ball for the Knicks," Doc says. "My big job is to be a father. It's the better job, but it's the harder job too, the more challenging. There is a lot of contrast between being an athlete and being a father. For example, at the end of a basketball game you know who won, who lost, who was injured, who played well. Clear results, right away. You don't know anything so sure after most events with kids—you do things you think will have good effects, but you don't really know right away. You have to watch them, see how they grow, see what needs doing, fixing, reinforcing. You have to feel what they are feeling, and sometimes that's very hard to do."

It is even harder if your kids are feeling whatever it is at bedtime in Connecticut and you are dribbling a basketball in Seattle, after having dribbled a basketball the night before in Minneapolis, before moving on to dribble a basketball the next night in Oakland. Spending time with the whole Rivers family shows that Doc is a good father, with a good degree of the natural attentiveness, tenderness, intuition, and sense of moment-to-moment responsibility many working fathers cannot discover so easily within themselves. But in order to deliver these goods, you have to be around.

"I can't pretend, to myself or Kris or the kids, that I am sharing all the home things all the time. Yes, my heart is always here, of course, but we all have to face the fact that Daddy is gone a lot. We have to adjust to that lifestyle, as a family. We can't get into this thing of 'Because Daddy brought home a nice present, he wasn't really away.' No—I was *away*. And a few times, after the toughest games, before the slap of reality, I may be sitting here, but I'm not home yet. But the reason I was away, or the reason I am concentrating on the games, is that I was fulfilling my responsibilities as a father, too."

Rivers explains the obvious: This job and its rewards are the best things he can do for the family in his father-as-provider role. Like most fathers, he would rather be playing Frisbee with his kids—or even changing their diapers—than working day in, day out. But he has a good job and he has to do it, for the kids as much as for his own satisfaction.

"Usually people have kids after they have started their professional lives; that's one of the reasons you feel it's a good time to start a family, because you have achieved a certain level of security. Same for Kris and me: I was doing pretty well in my career, we were happy, married, young—time to share all that with some children. You don't necessarily think, 'When we have kids, we will have to completely change everything so we can both be there all the time.' No one does that. It's just that in my case, 'going to the office' is extreme. The office is far away sometimes."

Rivers lifts a finger. "I cannot let it appear that I am some super father who regrets every minute he spends away from the kids, who hates working. It is tough being away, but I want it to be clear that I also *love* going to my 'office.' I feel comfortable out there on the floor, or in the locker room with my teammates. And sometimes when I am home, to prepare for the games I have to concentrate *before* the games, during time that I could be sharing with the family. So I am often not mentally 'at home'—I am here but not here. At the same time I can be a good father and a bad father. It's strange."

The kids can get a kind of unconscious revenge, though. Once, when he was home, Rivers overheard Jeremiah and a friend setting up to play a Nerf basketball game against each other in the basement. They were arguing about who got to be David Robinson and who got to be Charles Barkley.

"In my own house!" Rivers wails, laughing. "My own *kid*! I thought, 'Hey—can't one of you at least *pretend* to want to be your old man?' No way. If it hadn't been David and Charles, it would have been Scottie and Michael they wanted to be, or somebody else. That's when I knew for sure that I was an everyday ballplayer. And, at the same time, *not* an everyday father."

Kris Rivers says, "We didn't plan on any of this, but you can never really plan your life, especially if you are thinking ahead before you have children. Life with children is always going to be a surprise. That's one of the things that makes it so good. Our children are the best thing in our lives, the most important. But we did bring them into a life that was kind of underway, and there's nothing wrong with everyone living that life. We all live it together. We can't compare our life to some ideal and say, 'Here is where we fall short.' We make sure there is no falling short, in terms of our own lifestyle."

Still, there are some agonies, especially for the parents. "I get incredibly lonesome on the road," Doc says. "I miss Kris and Jeremiah and Callie and Austin. I call every day, but the phone is the phone. Sometimes, it is true, the peace and quiet of a hotel room is welcome. But most of the time, when I'm lying in a hotel bed in San Antonio or Portland, I wish I were here with kids all over me. But you can't feel sorry for yourself or for anyone else." He thinks for a moment. "The hardest thing for a parent is knowing when you miss something you can never get back. I have missed seeing each of my kids take his or her first step. I have missed hearing each kid say the first word. I have missed two first birthdays. That hurts. It's hard for me to say, 'That's the way it is—that's my life.' But I have to say that. My kids understand and accept it better than I do, I *hope*. It's pretty unfair for me to just *assume* they understand."

Kris and Glenn—and Callie, Austin, and Jeremiah—know Glenn will probably be away a lot for as long as he works. When asked if things will change when he retires as a player in a few years, both parents say "No" simultaneously. "This is our lifestyle," Kris says. Glenn adds, "If I coach, it will be the same. I love this game. I will always try to be involved in this game—coaching, broadcasting, management, whatever—and that means more of the same kind of motion and challenge. But I will still be doing the same as a father, too: loving my kids, and taking care of them in all the ways a man has to."

Rivers in for Rivers

On the Chicago playgrounds Glenn Rivers grew into a terrific player. He would walk all over the city—or occasionally ride with an older friend whose purpose in life was to scout out hot "runs" and shuttle younger players to them—to find the action. The action was worth the trouble, because the city boasted some tremendous basketball players: Fourteen of the guys he played with, on the playgrounds and in the informal Boys' Club league, went on to play in the NBA. They include Mark Aguirre, Darrell Walker, Ronnie Lester, Terry Cummings, Craig Hodges, Rod Higgins, and Isiah Thomas. Of these, Thomas is the best now, and was the best then— except, perhaps, for the young Rivers.

"We had a kind of rivalry," Doc says. "Nothing that made us enemies or anything. We knew each other, and our teams played each other. In fact, a playground game against Isiah's team remains one of the most memorable games of my life."

Rivers's pickup team against Isiah's pickup team ("Not our regular teams—just boys from the 'hood"): five-on-five, fullcourt, to thirty-two points by twos, win by four, other teams waiting to play winners, hustle up. But there was something different happening that day.

"We played a game. I don't remember which team won, but it was very close, probably 32–28. Great game, one of those times everyone is clicking. Even so, when it was over, we thought, 'Well, that was cool. Next?' But the guys waiting to play waved everyone back, told us to play again. Now, that *never* happened—you *never* gave up a game just to watch other guys play. But all the others were just standing there, quieter than usual, watching, and we felt something. So we played again. This time the team that lost the first game won, but it was just as close, 34–30 or something. When it was over, the same thing happened: 'Play again.' "

Rivers says he noticed a few more people had come, to watch. He and Isiah and their teammates turned back and played another great game, and once more were forbidden to stop, by a crowd that had gotten a little larger. They played, and played, and played.

"Every basket seemed to lead to a better one," he says. "Both teams were just running, hitting, practically floating. After a while we didn't even stop to check about continuing to go. We knew. We were playing great ball. Nobody on the court was getting tired or angry. Both teams wanted to win, but you could feel for once that instead of just five guys on one team making something coordinated happen, all *ten* of us were creating it together. It was . . . just basketball. But we had something, and nobody out there wanted it to end. Every now and then I would glance around, and there were more and more people watching. Word must have gotten around town, because people were showing up from everywhere. They were standing ten deep, they were hanging from the wire fence. I had never seen so many people watching a pickup game, but they were there, and they were *into* it. They were just standing there loving the game, loving basketball. So were we."

Eventually, after several hours, it was over. "I don't remember how it ended," Rivers says. "Isiah and I argue about it—I say *we* won more games than they did, he says they won more. This is *my* book, so here's the word: *We* won." He laughs. "In any case it ended just right. We played for hours, but we didn't play too long. Man, what we felt—we all just knew how great it was. The people watching went wild; they showed a kind of appreciation you don't see demonstrated that way on the playground. Everybody knows basketball pretty well out there, everybody recognizes a good move, a good play, but you never just *clap* or anything. It was great to hear."

And the next day, the usual playground routine resumed. To thirty-two by twos, win by four. Winners, teams waiting, hustle up. Later, in the NBA, it would be another routine—forty-eight minutes, win by whatever you can, millions watching, hustle up—but never would a game hum along in such a perfect flow and be understood so well by everyone playing and watching. Doc and Isiah would face off a hundred times; they would never reach the same spot they shared that day in Chicago.

But despite the competition available from great players who would one day be All-Americans, NBA All-Stars, even Hall of Famers, the contest Rivers most needed to win was, once more, a matter of family.

"My brother Gar was a pretty good player, and of course he was three years older than me," Doc says. "From very early in my days of playing ball, we played one-on-one. He did not take it easy on me; if I was going to challenge him, he was going to make me beat him at his best. So he killed me. It was three years before I scored my first *basket* against him. I remember running into the kitchen to tell my mother, 'Momma, I scored on Gar! I scored on Gar!' She looked at me and said, 'Um-hm, and what was the score of the game?' I told her it was 32–2. She said, 'Don't go bragging yet. You've got some work to do.'"

Rivers laughs, but his eyes say this is a serious subject. "I kept playing him. And I started to score more. This is years we are talking about. Eventually I was getting beat by only a few baskets, then by two, then the games would go on for a while, down one basket then tied, down one then tied, until he could get the margin up to two. And then one day, I finally did it." He sighs. "I was in the eighth grade. He was a junior. I remember the shot perfectly. I could do it step for step right now. I was up 30–28, I had the ball above the line, I pump-faked, and then I drove around him and scored a layup."

Rivers smiles grimly. "It was an amazing moment for me. I *beat* him! After *years* of being *killed*. It was *over*. I was ecstatic. I was going crazy, 'I won! I won! I won!' "

He shakes his head. "But my brother was too mad to take it. I see how he felt, but he was wrong, because what he did was to cheat. He said, 'No basket. You traveled.' I had not traveled. We both knew it. I argued. He insisted. Well—he was bigger than me, so I gave him the ball. He was cheating and he knew it as well as I did, and he couldn't stop himself. Getting beat by your younger brother was too much, when it finally happened. I think we both knew it would happen one day, but he wasn't ready. So we resumed the game. And he beat me. The moment was past."

A chance came for Gar to atone, for him gracefully to pass the torch. When he was a senior in high school, Gar was a starter for Proviso East, with a distinguished hoops career behind him. Glenn was a freshman, with a sparkling career ahead. The younger brother played most of the season with the freshman squad, but for the last few games he was brought up to the varsity. It was only the second time in the school's history that a freshman had been promoted; Glenn's only predecessor was his uncle, Jim Brewer.

"I was only sitting on the bench, but even so it was pretty unusual for a freshman to be up with the varsity. I mean, this was a school with an incredible tradition of basketball, in a city that takes the sport very seriously. Ask anyone about ball in Chicago! At Proviso East, every game was standing room only, the fans were very sophisticated about what happened on the floor, the team had media coverage you wouldn't believe for a high school. And it was extremely rare for a freshman to be brought into this: you had to start low and earn your way up. Well, I was good, I played well as a freshman, and I guess the coaches thought I had earned my way up a little early. So there I was. It was an honor just to sit. The fans appreciated it, even though I wasn't playing."

There he was, on the bench, as the season wound down. "Then one game, I remember we were playing Oak Park–River Forest, and I was sitting, watching my brother play, as usual. We had a big lead, and all of a sudden the coach got up and looked down the bench and said, 'Glenn. Go in for Gar.' "

Now Rivers cannot help smiling, a huge, warm one. "I went to the scorer's table. The announcer said, 'Glenn Rivers, in for Grady Rivers.' I trotted out on the floor. The place, the crowd, was going nuts, standing up, clapping, hollering, I don't know what. I went out on the floor and pointed at Gar and said, 'I got you.' Gar came over to me. I didn't know what he would do. But he grabbed me in a big hug, and he went to the bench. And I played. Every time I touched the ball, the fans screamed, 'Shoot! Shoot!' They wanted to see the freshman score, it was so unusual. I missed my first shot; then I drove around a guy and hit my next one, and the place went crazy again. I looked over, and Gar was jumping up and down with his arms in the air, going berserk. And that was it."

His smile won't fade. "If I had to choose, that was the *happiest* moment of my entire basketball career: following in my uncle's footsteps, coming in as a freshman for my brother, scoring my first basket. It was great. It was especially great because more than any person, Gar is responsible for me being a professional basketball player. We had a strange relationship, because we fought a lot growing up, but he always, *always* looked out for me, protected me, even from myself. He made a lot of wrong moves, and he knew it, and he was *not* going to let me make the same ones. He could have gone scholarship to a good school, but he didn't have the grades. He had to go to a junior college to get his grades up, and he told me, 'I will kill you if you let *your* grades go down.' He sometimes hung around with a bad crowd, and I wanted to hang out too, but he wouldn't let me. He would literally push me out of the car sometimes when he was hanging with someone he didn't want me to be around. I'd holler, but he'd say, 'Get out of here.' But most important, he played me hard all those years when he was better than me. He beat me and beat me and beat me, and I just got more and more determined and aggressive and confident. Gar was the main man, for me."

One question, though, still remains: Did he ever beat Gar one-on-one?

"Oh, yes," he laughs. "I beat him. It was that same year, when I was a freshman and he was a senior, and it was in the school gym in front of everybody. See, after practice people would always play games like that, and one day Gar and I went, and I beat him. And he was *furious*. After that we went back and forth, you know. But I started beating him more and more."

Zo

Of all the young guys in the league, the one I expect the most of is Alonzo Mourning," says Rivers. "Alonzo is special. He is going to be one of the greats. He needs to add a few things to his game, but he will. Everybody knows he is very weak going to his left, so in our play-off with Charlotte we forced him left, left, left the whole series. It worked up to a point, but by the last game he was tricking us by going left on his own a few times, and doing it with more control than he had shown before. That's a good sign.

"But Alonzo already has something far more important than any skills. He is the meanest man on the planet. He is as mean as any ten-year veteran gets after years of banging and growling and clawing his way through the league. Alonzo has the perfect attitude to win. He *hates* your sorry tail.

"In our series, there was one point when a Charlotte player was called for a foul, and Starks went to the line. Alonzo was lined up on the lane, and he was griping to the referee, 'He didn't foul him. He didn't foul him. He didn't foul him.' Over and over. *Mad.* I could see the ref getting angry. So, kind of being the nice old veteran, I said to Alonzo with a chuckle, 'Zo, I think he fouled him.' He turned on me with this absolutely ferocious look in his eye, incredulous that I would *dare* speak to him, and he glared at me like I was a cockroach. 'Who the bleep are *you*?' he said. 'Bleep *you*.' "

Rivers laughs. "It was fantastic. It was just what I deserved. I loved it. He's going to go a long way, Alonzo is. He's going to go wherever he wants."

Race

*T*he National Basketball Association is often held up as a sign that racism in the U.S. has pretty much been beaten. How else could a league composed mostly of black athletes be so beautifully accepted and loved throughout a country that is still mostly white? There is more than a little willful self-congratulation in this analysis—white people saying, "See? We let you play ball for us; we even pay you a lot of money to do so. We watch you on TV; we feature your black faces in advertisements for products we are trying to sell to white people! Aren't we bighearted? Haven't we come a long way?" There is more than a little false analogy at work too: that using a black star as a selling tool equates with fairly accepting anonymous black coworkers or costudents in the nitty-gritty increments of daily life.

"Oh, there is still racism in the NBA, and in society," says Rivers matter-of-factly. "Look at the upper management of teams, for example. We have some black coaches, but how many black general managers are there? There are a few, but usually they have a white team president or some other officer over them. This isn't necessarily because of hate-filled racism or anything like that; you can say that the owners, all of whom are white, are just hiring their friends, and their friends are, naturally, mostly white. Most of the time, hatred doesn't even come into it. It's being comfortable, trusting someone you know, or someone who has the same background. Most of them are white, so they hire mostly white guys. It's more a matter of subtle beliefs and inclinations that nudge you, small influences that lead you to make this choice or that. But it all adds up—to no black executives, no black people with all the power and responsibility. Because there is still the nagging feeling among many people that blacks cannot handle the brain work, they won't be completely responsible. Most white people probably aren't even aware they think this way—they would be shocked to hear this said about them, because most of them have very fine intentions and a strong outspoken commitment to fairness. But these deep feelings come into play."

Rivers speaks without visible anger, but without any accommodating humility, either: This is how it is, this is what we have to work with. If anything, he is grimly bemused by the persistent attitudes that dominant people cannot seem to recognize, despite their outspoken commitment.

"I could read a scouting report on any athlete, with his name removed, and tell you whether he was black or white, just by the comments made about him. If he is black, he is going to be 'athletically gifted ... quick ... great leaper ... with great instincts.' If he is white, he is going to be 'heady ... determined ... a take-charge guy ... a floor general.' It happens again and again; you can listen to any announcer on any station. It's wrong to do this, it's really misleading, but it never seems to strike anyone. Of course there *are* gifted black athletes who can really jump, and there are smart white guys. But the reverse is also true a lot of the time. And most important, an athlete's attributes have nothing to do with his color. But the media just will *not* mix the standard descriptions. Maybe the quickest guy in the league is Mark Price, but does anyone ever reduce Mark Price to that— 'He's quick, he's got that natural quickness'? No way—quickness is for black players. The smartest on-court player ever was Magic Johnson. Did you ever hear how intelligent Magic was at figuring defenses out? No—he had 'the natural instinct,' or something like that."

He laughs and sighs. "Actually, a great chance was lost when we failed to describe Larry Bird and Magic Johnson accurately. They were such a pair—they were the two best ever, and their careers matched each other, they played for all of those championships. If we had seen each of them for what he was and said so, we could have really smashed the stereotypes. Magic wasn't *that* quick, and he was not a super leaper, and he didn't have the smoothest shot, and some of his pure instincts—the reactions you can see in how a player plays defense, for example—were not all that great either. Magic always got a lot of steals, so people assume he was a terrific defender, but he wasn't. What Magic had was intelligence and incredible determination and a tremendous sense of responsibility, a very fine ability to analyze spontaneously, to take a game over through what he wanted to make happen. As for Larry—well, he *wasn't* slow. He had a lot of quickness; he was a *tremendous* athlete. He could jump enough to beat you to any rebound he wanted. And he had awesome instincts, with all those quick no-look passes over his shoulder and sudden three-pointers at exactly the right moment. If we had been forced to say so, we could have said Magic played more 'white' and Bird played more 'black.' But we never noticed. We just looked at the two of them, and called Magic quick and instinctive, and called Larry slow and smart and determined. Because they *looked* the parts. The message was almost subliminal, from the media: The highlight films of Magic show him making some cool pass, but the shots of Larry always show him diving for a loose ball or doing something that says 'hard worker.' Hey, Magic worked just as hard. But that doesn't come across."

One thing in the racial stereotyping does anger Rivers. "I hate it, really hate it, when people make fun of what they see as ignorance. When they mock an athlete for what they define as being 'dumb.' It's mostly a racial thing, though part of it represents a general prejudice against athletes. Mostly, though, you hear it about black players. They are crude and physical, rather than intelligent. They speak poorly, with awful grammar. They can't think; they can only master superficial physical skills that mean nothing, skills that reflect no cleverness or anything like that."

Rivers shakes his head. "Well—first of all, as far as language goes, it is true that some athletes don't have a great command of grammar. But most of these guys had no trouble getting good grades from college teachers, in English and everything else. How come? Well, it was because the teachers, all the way back to elementary school probably, felt they had to pass the athletes without forcing them to learn anything. They thought they were doing them a favor: 'This kid doesn't know anything, but he can really shoot the ball, so here's a B.' The further along the kid got, the less he knew compared to everybody else, so the more his passing depended on pure gifts from the teacher. So all of a sudden one day you have a twenty-five-year-old man with a college degree and he can barely read, and somebody grabs him and puts him in front of a TV camera and asks him a question. So he says, 'The Knicks be saying we scared of them but we ain't got no fear of *nobody* . . .' and everybody just nods and says, 'Just what we always knew: Black athletes are dumb.' "

Rivers says the paucity of black sports reporters keeps certain misunderstandings alive. "It's not racism that there are few black reporters," he says, "but the fact is, white reporters often fail to understand the differences between a white guy and a black guy. A black athlete says or does something that is accepted in black culture, but the white reporter misinterprets it and writes it up as something bad. Or the white guy mocks the differences, mocks the black way of doing or saying something, all because he doesn't understand it. Well, there's no way we can expect him to understand it; but at the same time, he should learn to accept differences without feeling he has to judge them. Moses Malone is the perfect example. Moses is *not* a dumb guy. He is not a 'problem player,' either. He has been a leader everywhere he has played, he has willingly taught younger players, and he has worked harder than anybody. But because he speaks in black slang that white reporters don't understand, he is mocked as being stupid. And his feelings get hurt, and he acts cranky, and the press gets cranky right back, and the next thing you know all everyone knows about Mo is that he's a 'problem.' It's all wrong. In Mo's case it's a big shame, because here is one of the greatest players ever to play the game. *Ever*. But will there be a farewell tour when Moses retires? City after city throwing a Mo party, giving him presents? No way. Nobody's going to give Moses a car every night. Because of the way he has been portrayed, through misunderstanding arising from racial differences."

The worst instances of racial labeling, Rivers says, are those in which a black athlete is scorned for doing something a white guy gets away with. "For example, say there's a white athlete who says wild things to the press, does crazy things in and out of the locker room, pulls pranks on teammates, acts weird on the field. Well, he's a 'free spirit,' right? Bill Lee, the old Red Sox pitcher. He's 'creative,' or 'a real joker' or 'fun loving,' and it's assumed there's some overall reasoning behind his acting up. People spoke of him with a smile, 'Oh, he marches to his own drummer.' But a black guy who does the same sort of stuff is 'an attitude problem.' Like Dick Allen. He's just *strange* and *dangerous*. Nobody ever assumes there's an intelligence at work behind the act. Nobody smiles when they speak of Dick Allen."

The perfect example of this sort of double standard is Bill Walton. Walton was a great champion at UCLA, and he led Portland to a championship in 1977, his third season; at the end of his career, he was a reserve on a Celtic championship team. Rivers dislikes stats, but some may be pertinent: Walton missed four *entire* seasons with injuries, and in four others he played in only ten, fourteen, thirty-three, and thirty-five games; his average number of games played per season was thirty-three! He has fewer rebounds—*thousands* fewer—than James Donaldson or Mark

Eaton, to name two. Darrell Walker and Charles Oakley have more career points, and Walton's scoring average—13.3—matches Bill Laimbeer's (Laimbeer's is higher for the play-offs). As far as his presence and character go, he was the definitive "free spirit"—always making naïve political proclamations, claiming to be the victim of crass cultural and medical conspiracies, trumpeting his parvenu membership in the '60s generation that he had missed the first time around, quitting his team, suing his team, issuing ultimatums at press conferences so he might be induced to re-sign. . . . He was a classic total wacko. But he was just elected to the NBA Hall of Fame. On the first ballot.

Rivers laughs. "It's ridiculous! I mean—*Earl Monroe* didn't make it on the first ballot! Earl Monroe! Is Walton there because he was a great college player? Is that what the Hall of Fame is for? Okay, that's fine, Bill Walton deserves it—but where are players like Austin Carr, who was astounding in college, had a few great pro seasons, but was never himself because of injuries? Where is Adrian Dantley? I'm not saying there was a conscious racial decision: 'We got to get this white man in here!' I *am* saying that Walton, as a white guy, received some major breaks from the voters, enjoyed the benefits of some relaxed standards. Walton represented something to a lot of people—the 'Great White Hope' thing, I guess—and that is why he is a Hall of Famer now. I'd like to point out that it's not what I call 'racism'—it's just rooting for someone you can identify with. But that doesn't make it right. As for being a 'free spirit'—well, I guess all is forgiven, especially if you get a job on TV. That's fine—but let's just see how long it takes them to forgive Moses Malone for *his* 'free spiritedness.' "

Rivers returns to the "dumb" stereotype. "The poor-language thing with athletes is just a sign of how badly these guys were prepared. Now, you can correct the language thing on the surface, and get away with a lot. Take me, for example. My college coach, Hank Raymonds, forced all his athletes to take speech classes so that at least we could *sound* smart. And I am aware that I am one of those athletes the media have learned to look to for comments that sound all bright and educated. This is not because I am smarter than anybody else. It is because I decided to work very hard on my speech, my language. And let me tell you, it is hard as hell. I resent it at times, how difficult it is for me to keep learning how to speak well, and to stay on top of myself and not get sloppy. The reason it is so hard is that I have not been prepared by my education; I never learned the fundamentals. I blame no one but myself—some of those teachers *wanted* to teach me. And I pay for it, every day. So I have to work extra hard now. I grew up with respect for language, largely because my father, a black cop, was a reader. He was reading a book every day of his life when I was at home; I'm sure he still is. That didn't make *me* read and study, but it must have taught me some respect, because it is important to me now."

Rivers points to the notebook that holds his monthly schedule. "This summer I have arranged with a writing teacher to take a class in grammar. Basic grade-school grammar, the kind *you* learned in the third grade, fourth grade, fifth grade. I don't know it. I sound okay most of the time, but I don't know the rules. I'm thirty-two years old and I am catching up on fifth-grade work. I am not dumb—I just missed some things. Because I never *had* to do them. People kept doing me the 'favor' of passing me along."

Rivers explains once again that there are all kinds of people playing basketball in the NBA—some smart, some not so smart, some articulate, some not so articulate, as in any field or profession. There are some brilliant people—he mentions Patrick Ewing—but their brilliance isn't likely to be shown to the casual observer. But in general, he says, pro basketball players deserve credit for a kind of intelligence no one thinks to appreciate.

"Every time I hear someone crack a joke about a dumb athlete, I say: 'Look: This man is at the absolute top of his field. This is as high as he can go in the entire world, in the work of his choice. He has figured out a pretty complicated job, and he does it in the face of incredible pressure and competition. He has a Ph.D. in basketball. How can you say he is a dummy? Dummies don't get that far.'

"Even the guys you wouldn't think were so thoughtful and bright—the pure shooters, for example. They *seem* to be nothing but instinct and talent. But somebody like Otis Birdsong, somebody like Randy Wittman—those guys were pretty slow, not big, not 'great athletes,' but they were *always open*. There were nine other guys scurrying around in the halfcourt, covering almost the whole floor, but Otis and Witt always found a spot they could shoot from, unchallenged. They watched one guy moving that way, and saw where this other guy's path would intersect this third guy, and how that would create a little pocket of space right *here* just about *now* . . . and the ball would come and *koosh!* Two points.

"So tell me: How did they always figure it out, if they weren't some kind of engineers? That's what it was, really—it was engineering. It was physics: motion, time, space. Pure physics. Not calculated in a laboratory with all the time in the world. It was spontaneous physics, it was calculated on the spot. But it was no less brilliant than what a physicist might do with a blackboard and a bunch of math formulas." He shakes his head. "There is a difference between being uneducated and being dumb. 'Uneducated' means you just didn't get the instruction. There's a lot you didn't get the chance to know, or didn't *take* the chance to know. But like these guys, you may be very smart about the things you *do* know. As for 'dumb'—well, that's nothing but a putdown."

If the world at large doesn't give such abilities the credit they deserve, certainly a player's teammates do. In fact, it is only the players themselves who know what they do every day. And they appreciate each other with a generous pride and a fierce defensiveness. And, according to Rivers, they are also completely colorblind.

"The *team*, the twelve players—now *there* is a model for a just society," he says. "The problems at the upper levels and so on don't exist among the teammates. Competition destroys all sense of color. We are in this task together and we are completely dependent on each other, and we are absolutely pulling for each other every minute. A guy simply will never think, 'I can't pass to that black guy!' or 'I have to get more rebounds than that white guy!' *Never*. We mix in every way. Sometimes it seems we completely forget or just don't see any differences between ourselves; other times, it's more like we recognize the differences but in the spirit of appreciation, of enjoying how interesting differences can be. But on the floor, in the locker room, the plane, the hotel—color doesn't exist."

But the team cannot forget that the color of each player matters a great deal to the world at large, even when black players are invited to play golf or go to parties at places where other non–sports-star people of color are turned away. Rivers tells a long story about the partial boycott of a Mike Fratello Christmas party in Atlanta, a party one of the coach's friends scheduled at an all-white, anti-Semitic country club without Fratello's knowledge. It turned into an ugly citywide issue, with no one looking good: Fratello was embarrassed, players who attended were sheepish, Rivers, who inspired the boycott along with Jewish GM Stan Kasten, was depicted as being ungrateful and out of step with the joys of the season. The black players were supposed to be *honored* that the all-white club had let down its guard for the night, had allowed them into the sanctum. Instead, they got all uppity . . .

"I have no doubt that in many ways it is very healthy for a mostly white country to be pulling so sincerely for teams that are mostly black," Rivers says. "A white kid who wants to be Michael Jordan—well, that has to be having some good effect on that kid's sense of race. But, funny as it sounds, the benefits of the black league in a white land are diminished by the fact that to a lot of people a black athlete stops being black when he receives the adoration of white fans. It's like he's something else, not 'just a black' anymore. Michael is simply not seen as a black man by millions of people. He has 'transcended' his race. It has even happened to me. There was a white guy I knew in Atlanta who told me he wanted his son to grow up and be just like me. He seemed to mean it, and I was kind of embarrassed, but it was a nice thing to say, to feel. However, a week or so later when I was invited to play golf at his club, I found out they don't allow black members. I could be the role model for this guy's son, but if I wanted to join his club, I was suddenly just a black man and the answer was *get out*. How can you hold both feelings at the same time, unless you ignore my race on the one hand while looking at nothing *but* my race on the other?"

Rivers thinks for a moment. "Look. I am a man, first, but I *am* a black man, and that's it—that's not just *what* I am, it's *who* I am. I'm married to a white lady. We come from two totally different backgrounds and cultures. When we got together, it upset many people, especially Kris's boyfriend, who was an acquaintance of mine. I believe what upset him most was not that he lost his girl, but to whom. It's funny, I never thought I would be married; if so, I thought it would be to someone of the same background and culture as my own. But my parents taught me love is love. It shouldn't be love-if-you-are-black, or -white. Does that make the love tougher? Yes. Could I be naïve? Maybe. That is not a reason to run. Because if you do, then you have given in to hatred and ignorance. Ignorance does not admit the value of differences. But I believe in differences too. And sometimes the differences are going to have to lead me to stand up for something, when someone is trying to do something wrong. That's how it was with the Christmas party; someone we all liked was doing something wrong, and I had to stand up against it. I did not say anyone else should join me, but I did say each guy should do what felt *right* to him. At the time, Jon Koncak was the only white guy on the team, and he said, 'This doesn't concern me. It's up to you guys, and I'll go along with whatever you decide.' I said, 'No, Jon—it *does* concern you, because this is an issue of right and wrong, and right and wrong doesn't belong just to the particular group suffering the slight. And don't just go along with the group—use your *own* sense of what feels right.' It was hard to do. Again, we all liked Mike, we all liked the friend of Mike's who was the club member throwing the party, and so it was tough to turn on them."

Rivers notes with frank pride that the Hawks' partial boycott attracted enough attention to all-white clubs that the city of Atlanta almost immediately passed an ordinance stipulating that liquor licenses would henceforth be linked to color-blind membership policies. Exclude on the basis of race or religion, and you couldn't drink. "I loved it. I was very pleased to see how the city responded. It was worth a lot of anguish to get that response," he says.

"Here is something important for black kids to realize: It's easy to be black and 'stand up' when all it means is wearing the hip clothes and speaking the hip language and listening to the hip music. But standing up—if you are black or *white*—when someone is doing something wrong, especially when your stand is going to hurt someone you like—well, that's a lot harder. But you have to do what is right, whenever a chance requires it. Martin Luther King said that even if you are in the minority about perceiving what is right, you have got to *do* what is right."

The mention of King brings Rivers to a consideration of one of the three men he calls his idols: King, Arthur Ashe, and Muhammad Ali.

"Unfortunately, I first heard of Martin Luther King on the day he was killed. I was just a little kid, and I came home from school, probably first or second grade, and my parents and all my relatives were sitting around *crying*. I couldn't understand why. So they told me: A man named Dr. King had been shot. This made me interested in him, the fact that somebody wanted to shoot him, and did, and the fact that his death made so many people so far away unhappy. So I started to read stuff, and listen to old speeches. He was a strong man, and he had a strong line. I think he's very misunderstood, because people associate him with nonviolence and figure he must have been weak or wavering. He was non-violent, but he was *active:* He didn't hesitate to go to the front lines of battle, or to break the law when the law was in the way of right. He never fled from confrontation; he just wanted to keep the confrontation on a level that made you face your own argument and beliefs, instead of a level where the man with the bigger weapon would win without having to think.

"Malcolm X was misunderstood too. He is known for teaching violence. That's *not* what he taught. He taught that if you are hit, to hit *back;* he never said you should go out and gun down people. Yes, before he went to Mecca, he said he did not know if white people and black people could really get along, and he did say white people were often evil. But he changed his mind later, which is a pretty courageous thing for a man in his position to do. He felt he had to follow what was right too."

Rivers says one of his favorite principles of Dr. King is the advocacy of a peaceful response to an act of offense, "instead of a response that lowers you to the level of the person attacking you." He laughs. "That's what I forgot in the Kevin Johnson incident in Phoenix last year. KJ—and he's not a bad guy, the work he does with kids is tremendous—KJ gave me a cheap shot. I failed to control myself. I chased him right down to his level, instead of staying above it, staying *right*. The guys I look up to would not have wanted me to hit back. I should have just beaten KJ on the court; then he would have looked like even more of a fool for throwing that punch. Dr. King said if a guy hits you in the face and calls you a nigger, you look back at him and say, 'That's all right. I'm a *proud* nigger. I love myself. I even love *you*.' Then you leave, and he goes home, and he is even *more* furious. But eventually he realizes he's ashamed. He feels like a fool. From the *inside*. Because you didn't stoop."

Winding his way back to the subject of an NBA team's harmony, Rivers says, "Stooping isn't necessary there, because that kind of attack doesn't happen. Yes, sure, there are misunderstandings sometimes, and we might retreat into our comfort zone of racial explanation, 'He's wrong because he's white' or 'He's wrong because he's black.' But what athletes have in common is much more important than any ways in which they are different. So they are not afraid of the differences—they have no fear of each other. Athletes, black or white, are different from people in other walks of life. We understand each other, black or white. We have a bond. So, as teammates, when we share the exact same goal and commitment, then we agree on everything that is important."

The Footwork King

To me, the big player with the best moves in the history of the game was Kevin McHale. I mean it. The very best pivot man. Right behind him is Hakeem, but his moves aren't as good as Kevin's. The man had more dang moves—he could do it all, the whole repertoire. Up and under, fadeaway, sideways shots, anything you'd ever seen and a lot you hadn't. You never knew what was coming. You always guessed wrong. He was a *nightmare* for guys to guard. He could foul *anybody* out of a game. He fouled me out of quite a few, and I wasn't even the man supposed to *guard* him!

"It was all based on footwork. Get your feet right and your body will follow. Everything you do with your body *depends* on where your feet are, when you turn or jump. McHale was the greatest example of this—you could say he knew all the secrets of footwork. Even the most talented player could study the way Kevin moved his feet, set his feet, and that player could learn forever.

"He must have worked *hours* on every move. Here's a big, gangly, skinny, caved-in-chest guy, doesn't look like he has an athletic bone in his entire *body*. But he was an incredible athlete. The best moves ever—even the reverse dribble and stuff like that. He drove us crazy. We could never figure out when to trap him, when to double-team. He knew we couldn't figure him out, and he'd talk to you about it. He'd get next to me on the free-throw lane during a foul shot by somebody, he's getting ready to box me out, and he'd say, 'So—when're you guys going to trap today? You gonna trap before the pass, or on the pass, or are you waiting for me to do my move?' He'd laugh, and he'd be right to laugh. Because sure enough, if we trapped early, he'd get clear and be by the two of us to receive the pass. If we trapped on the pass, he'd dish off and a guy would get a layup. If we waited, he'd make his move and make you foul him.

"I got the ugliest fouls of my career, the most inept fouls, against Kevin McHale. I was always the guy who would come down to help out on the trap, and I could never figure out which way he was going to go, or when. I must have simply *run into* him twenty times in my career. And that's embarrassing, running into a guy— that's goofy. I know Fratello was always saying, 'What is wrong with Doc? He just ran into the guy!' But it was timing, and deception. McHale was a master."

Team D

*I*n today's NBA, Rivers faces some fierce challenges. He often guards Jordan, especially in the fourth quarter, and has done so for much of their careers. At one time or another, he will also cover John Stockton, Tim Hardaway, Kevin Johnson, Isiah Thomas, Mark Price, Steve Smith, Clyde Drexler—all players who probably bring more pure talent to the contest than he does. But he yields nothing to them, for all of their gifts.

"On the night I am covering a Michael Jordan, I must feel I can be better than Michael Jordan," Rivers says coolly. "I must look him in the eye before the tipoff and know that. On the night I am covering a KJ, same thing. The same goes for all of these guys. I can beat them all, on a given night, and the night when one of them is my man *is* the night. I look at him and know that I have to be smarter, tougher, more determined, whatever—that's how I start every game. How else am I going to be able to accept the assignment from the coach? I can't go out on the floor with the attitude that I am less of a player than my man, with the certainty that my man is going to kill me. The night I feel that way is the night I am doomed."

Rivers is a realist: He says he knows that all of these guys may be better than he is. "But on the night I guard them, I try to do one of two things: I will play to their level, or I will bring them down to mine. Sometimes I am successful. Sometimes I am not. I have held Michael Jordan to ten points in some games, and I have held him to sixty in others. Same with Isiah and the rest of them."

As Rivers explains, it's clear the conviction that he is better than a more-talented player on this or that night is not arrogance. It is self-respect: He knows he can depend on himself to rise to the task. He has done so for ten years, especially as a defender. "I *love* defense," he says. "That's where I'm going to get you."

In professional golf there is a saying, "Drive for show, putt for dough." The NBA could have a similar slogan to emphasize the crucial role of defense, so often obscured by the show of scoring. Beyond the blocked shot and the steal, tight defense is hard for fans to see, except on the scoreboard. But on the night of a seventh game in a championship series, give a coach the choice between a player who will score ten points more than his average and a player who will hold the other team's best scorer ten points below *his* average, and chances are he'll take the defender.

For an individual and a team, defense can be relied upon; it can be the consistent element in a game, a series, and a season, holding things steady until the scorers find their touch. Your scoring can be streaky, fluky, lucky, but your defense—if you are a very good defender—is not prey to such variations. It will be a little different every night, because you are guarding a different man. Overall it can achieve a very inspiring regularity.

How do the players known for their great defensive ability— and Rivers is one of them—become so terrific? Most players who make it to the NBA were big scorers in high school and junior high. Presumably, before that they were trying to be big scorers on the playgrounds where practically everyone in America learns the game. Putting the ball in the hole is the way you show off as a kid; when you inhibit a scorer with decent D, you're not exactly stand-ing out as an individual. On most playgrounds, teams are picked game by game, players recombining constantly, so an individual identity is all you have. Who is going to settle for a silent pride in the subtle art of defense, a triumph known only to himself and the shooter he frustrates?

"To start with, a good player knows defense is part of the game, and a good player wants to be good at everything," Rivers says. "If you're a hot scorer and there's one guy in your neighborhood you play against a lot who messes you up every time, you notice. He makes you dread playing against him. And before long you think, I'd like to be able to do that too. I'd like people to dread *me*."

At some point, though, a coach pitches in. Defense, according to Rivers, is probably the part of the game that depends the most on teaching, or at least responds most to it. This is largely because defense is a team business. You can be a great one-on-one defender, but unless your teammates help you out within the team concept, you can be diverted from your duty by all kinds of offensive team strategies, from picks to decoys. When a great playground player lands on his first organized team, he begins to learn how to play D, and from the beginning he is taught that his teammates are depending on him, as he is on them. When he is picked off his man, someone will jump over and cover for him. He will get his turn to do the same.

"I have had great coaches for defense," Rivers says. "From elementary school right up into the NBA. Mike Fratello in Atlanta was a very fine defensive teacher and coach. He opened a lot of guys' eyes to defense. But sometimes it was almost like he knew *too* much: He tried to control too much from the bench when we weren't executing the particular plan he had devised for that game. Playing for Pat Riley last year taught me a different way for a team to play defense. You build a team defensive scheme based on your team strengths, on the things your players can do best with the greatest consistency and confidence, then you go out and play that defense eighty-two times. Let the other teams' offenses adjust to *you*. Mike, in contrast, tried to get the Hawks to adjust to *them* every night. But here *we* set the conditions. This is what the '93

Knicks did, and it was awesome. We just *knew* we could stop anybody. Even Chicago, in the play-offs. We did not lose to Chicago because they beat our defense. They did not beat our defense. We missed free throws, and they didn't. That was the difference in a very close series."

Rivers holds up a finger. "No excuses from us. The Bulls responded as the champions they are. They did what it takes to win. They deserved it."

With a mixture of pride and pain Rivers recalls three critical Chicago possessions in the fourth quarter of Game Six, when the Knicks bollixed the Bulls into forcing long, off-balance three-pointers with only a couple of seconds left on the twenty-four-second clock. "That's what you work hard for twenty-two seconds to do," he says. "Make 'em take a bad shot." In these three instances, however, the bad shots went in. "Nothing more we could do, except give credit to Scottie Pippen and John Paxson. Those were some incredible shots to hit, at those moments. Coach Riley would love to have them take those shots all night. But with the confidence those guys had—who knows, they might hit most of them."

Defense brings us back, as always with Rivers, to the *team*. Defense in the NBA, at its best, when all five players are jumping from one man to the next in double-teams, switches, help-outs, is a marvelous act of teamsmanship; there is nothing better in any sport, as far as coordination and mutual commitment go. But such a defense comes very close to violating one of the NBA's cornerstone rules: Players must play man-to-man defense, each guarding a single opponent rather than covering an area of the court in a zone defense, picking up anyone who enters it, passing anyone leaving it along to the next defender, etc. It's an old rule, and basketball fans have made a myth out of it—there is something kind of dishonest, weak, sneaky, and unmasculine about playing D in such a way that you need to rely on your teammates for help. The man-to-man rule seems to say: Here in the big leagues, we go head to head. Two gunslingers in the noonday sun, no help. Draw!

This imagery has its appeal. But the fact is, a team that plays five simultaneous one-on-one matchups, according to the strict letter of the rule and its apparent spirit, is going to get beat. Offenses can simply run too many defenders off their men. So, to win, players have to help each other. Your guy gets away from you, no problem, I'll pick him up for a few seconds if you'll pick up *my* guy or at least stand in the way of a potential pass to him. The fact is, each guy on a great defensive team plays man-to-*men*. No one is alert merely to his own assignment.

Watching five Knicks or five Bulls as they scramble and smother and trap and steal as if directed by one nervous system, a fan has to believe that in their wisdom the rule makers foresaw such a fulfillment of basketball's team ideal, though the rule itself seems to stipulate the opposite. The game's inventors and codifiers must have known that NBA players would grow to be like tax lawyers, finding every loophole and shady area, taking advantage of any bit of leeway in the enforcement, coming as close as possible to breaking the law. The refs do make calls against illegal defenses, but these are pretty much just to let coaches and players know they are watching. Someone like Rivers or Jordan, well known for anticipating passes and picking them off by leaping into a passing lane at the right moment, will get away with leaving his man to cover a spot. But a more impetuous player who jumps into the lanes too early too often, preventing passes rather than stealing them, will be nailed for guarding the floor instead of the man. Success breeds a certain immunity.

Some defenders are so talented they don't need any help. Rivers tells a story about the player he says is his all-time favorite, Maurice Cheeks. "When I was a rookie with Atlanta, we were getting ready to play the 76ers and Cheeks and I were going to guard each other. Johnny Davis gave me a tip about Maurice. He said, 'Don't try to throw a two-handed overhead pass by him. He'll get both of his hands up and catch it.' Well, I laughed. No way! It's true that pass gives the defender an extra half-second to see what you're going to do, but the force of the pass always makes up for that. You really whip that ball, and *nobody* standing practically chest to chest with you can get his hands up in time to catch it." Rivers shakes his head. "Well, there we were, Maurice and me, and he was guarding me close, and Dominique got open underneath. So I pulled the ball over my head—extra fast, because of what Johnny had said, even though I didn't really believe him—and I snapped it toward Nique, extra fast. *Skoosh!* Next thing I knew Maurice was busting past me dribbling the ball upcourt for a layup. He had done it—he had gotten both of his hands up, and not only *up*, but up and in the right position and with the right touch to *catch* the ball. I mean, it would have been awesome enough if he had just deflected it. But to just pluck it out of the air like that . . . Well, I never did it again. But I saw him burn guard after guard through the years."

Magic

Doc says, "When Magic Johnson would start playing with a new guy, he would throw the guy passes the guy could reach with his hands if he hustled. For a trial period, Magic would presume the guy could run and catch and understand that Magic was using the ball to lead him to the spot where he *should* be, from which he could score more easily than any other spot. A smart player like James Worthy would catch on, and say, 'Wherever you want, Magic,' and would just go where Magic led him. Catch the ball and put it in, and your shooting percentage is suddenly five-sixty and thank you very much, Magic.

"But not everybody caught on. Some of them resisted, or they were slow, or they had bad hands, or they just refused to believe they could actually hustle to the spots Magic was leading them. So after they missed a few passes, Magic would say to himself, 'If that's the way you want it, kid, then maybe you can catch one in your face.' And from that point on he would pass the ball directly at the man's face."

Rivers laughs. "Now, Magic threw the ball *hard*. His passes had a lot of touch, they could be handled easily, but they came at you like a rocket. A basketball moving that fast is like a small boulder; it will break your nose in a flash. Magic knew very well that *anyone* can get his hands up to protect his face from getting smashed. So he used that reflex to make these guys catch his passes. If you flunked his test—if you didn't hustle to the balls you could reach with your hands fully extended in front of you—then from that point on you saw nothing but passes coming at your eyes. And you caught them. And *then* you put the ball in the hole. Probably you wished you had done what Magic was showing you to do the first time around."

Competition

I think a guy's game will usually reflect his personality," says Doc. "There's a natural relationship between the two, of course. What you see on the court is what you get in the man. It's true that sometimes the style of play seems to be related to the man kind of as an opposite—say, when a guy who seems shy and quiet plays fierce and fiery. But really that just means there's something fiery hidden inside him."

Well, then there's certainly something fiery inside Rivers. He is Atlanta's all-time leader in technical fouls, for example, and he had two well-publicized scraps in 1993, with Kevin Johnson and Isiah Thomas. And then there was the shouting fury he drew from Michael Jordan in Game Six of the conference finals. . . . "I have to live a kind of contradiction," he says. "On the court, I *am* a fiery person, almost a mean person. I feel absolutely cutthroat sometimes, which is *good* in competition. Off the court, I'm not like that; I try to be a nice guy. It's my job to master the cutthroat side and let it out at the right time, on the basketball floor. Sometimes I slip, and lose my temper at the wrong time. My fiery self jumps out when it shouldn't. When I was a kid, I didn't know I needed to pick and choose and control. I let the fire rage whenever it flared up. But getting that under control is a large part of growing up."

Rivers shrugs. "It all comes down to emotion. As a player, I had to face something long ago: I am simply not talented enough to play without emotion," he says. "To play well in this league, you have to be completely into the game, into the moment. It's a matter of concentration, but not just the kind of mental concentration you muster when you have the time, like on the free-throw line. The concentration that carries you through a game entirely on the *inside* is something less calculated. For me, that means emotion. It's part determination, part anger, part confidence—there's a lot to it, but it all comes down to *feeling* it. Sometimes, if I don't feel it, if I'm slipping in and out of the rhythm of the game, I will do something artificial to stimulate myself emotionally. Maybe I'll yell at a ref about a call—kind of invent some anger to get me going. But most of the time I don't need to do anything. The pure competition is enough."

"Competition" is one of those words—like "team"—that Rivers speaks with a glow, a reverence. When he talks about competition, you feel there is a great deal more richness to it than most of us know. He laughs when he is told that his wife Kris says he has gotten more competitive as the years go by. He agrees with her analysis that this is partly because his goals have gotten increasingly difficult to achieve. First, Kris explains, he just wanted to be drafted high (he went thirty-first overall in 1983). Then he wanted to make the Hawks, just be on the team. Then he wanted to play a lot; then to start; then for his team to win a lot; then for his team to do well in the play-offs. Now there is only one goal: He wants his team to win the NBA championship. That happens to only 12 players a year, whereas when he wanted to be a starter, for example, he wanted to join a group of about 120. When you have to beat almost everyone in the league to reach your goal, you get tougher and smarter and more ferocious year by year.

You also get older. Rivers acknowledges that being increasingly fiery has a lot to do with being increasingly aged. "The clock is ticking," he says, "and I hear it. Almost everyone does, including the people who play against you."

LEFT: Glenn and Gar, before the one-on-one wars, circa 1965. *Courtesy Glenn Rivers*

BELOW: A great scorer in the Proviso East tradition. *Courtesy Glenn Rivers*

LEFT: The jersey says it all (with John Wooden). *Norm Fisher/California Photo Service*

Rick Majerus and head coach Hank Raymonds (back row, first and second left) taught many lessons that stuck with Doc (middle row, second left). *Courtesy Glenn Rivers*

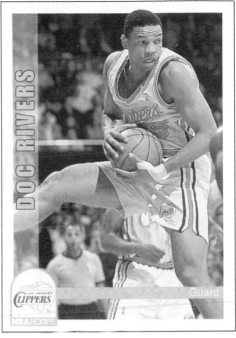

Long a Hawk, briefly a Clipper, and a Knick forever.
NBA Properties, Inc.

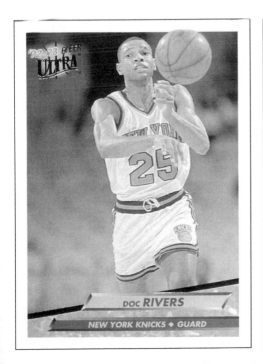

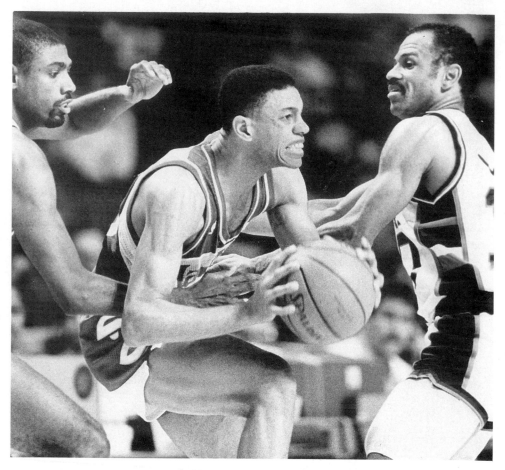

"I have to play with emotion." *Gary Weber/Non-Stop Images*

"I always get up for the play-offs." *Millan Manuel/Sports Illustrated*

It's over. *New York Times*

Teammates, 1992–93: (seated left to right) Bo Kimble, Hubert
Davis, Greg Anthony, coach Pat Riley, Doc, Rolando Blackman,
John Starks; (standing left to right) Tony Campbell, Eric Anderson,
Herb Williams, Patrick Ewing, Charles Smith, Charles Oakley,
Anthony Mason. *George Kalinsky/Major League Graphics*

"Always do what you can for kids—whether you're teaching them something or just saying hello. You never know when a small word from you is going to make a big difference to them."
Top: *Courtesy Glenn Rivers*
Bottom: *George Kalinsky/Major League Graphics*

Three generations of Riverses:
Doc and his parents,
Grady senior and Betty;
Doc and Kris;
Jeremiah, Callie, and Austin.
Courtesy Glenn Rivers

But sometimes your younger teammates don't. At one point last year Rivers took the step of addressing the team and letting them listen to the ticks: He reminded his teammates that they *knew* they had a team that could win the championship, and that they should seize it now instead of taking their time. It is rare for him to strike a pose, but he did so: He was The Noble Veteran With Few Chances Left, Drawing Today's Youth Into Focus.

It was not a false pose. "I told them I had spent my career trying to get to the point we were closing in on. I had never been so close. I knew I would not have many more or better opportunities. I wasn't about to sit by and let any *kids*"—he smiles at his officiousness—"any Young Players Who Thought They Had Forever, let this chance slip away. Patrick and I told them: We want it now."

The Knicks didn't get it now. ("And it was *not* the kids' fault," he insists. "We all let ourselves down. Before we let any fan down, we let ourselves down, all together.") It will take Rivers more than a few months to get over the missed chance. During the off-season, whenever a well-wisher said, "Great year you guys had!" he gently demurred: "Well, it was a *good* year. But definitely not a *great* one." This left a lot of well-wishers scratching their heads. But Rivers, despite his gratitude for support and appreciation, was still spitting out the grit of defeat that would be bitter forever.

"The great thing about basketball is that it's such a complete team game. You come to appreciate this more as you play more; you come to *love* it. It's what makes you excited to go out on the floor at the start of a game. You aren't going to have to do it alone; you're going to be a part of something bigger than you are. Baseball is a team game, with each player doing his part, and they all add up, a base hit, a walk, a sacrifice bunt, a fly ball . . . but the individual actions are done alone, and then they add up in time. In basketball you make it happen, all together, all at once. It's great. It's just like realizing when you grow up how rich it is to be part of a family. So, anyway, it stands to reason that when you get further along in your career, when this teamwork means more and more to you, the only achievements that mean anything are the team achievements. And there's only one great team achievement."

Fans who watch the winning players exult at the end of the championship series every spring will be surprised to learn that any NBA player ever wants anything *else*. But there are those whose dreams don't extend so far. Rivers says the 1993 Knicks were the first of his teams to express a man-by-man commitment to the single goal of winning it all.

What?

"That's right," he says. "In a team meeting at the beginning of the season each guy was asked what his goal for the year was. Every player said, 'The championship.'" Rivers seems pleased.

But isn't that what every player says every year?

"Not at all," he says. "You get guys who say, 'I want to make the All-Star team,' or 'I want to average eight rebounds a game,' or 'I want to achieve what's in my incentive clauses.'"

They *admit* such things? In front of the coach? Surely they at least *pretend* they want a team goal.

He shakes his head. "Not always. Oh, sure, sometimes, if a few guys say they want to win it all, the next guy will say the same thing. But everyone can tell he's putting it on. We all know each other pretty well. You can tell what a guy has in mind, what a guy is shooting for, whether it's a scoring title and a new contract or the championship. Of course we are all professionals; of course anyone would rather win than lose, even just for purely selfish reasons. In fact there's nothing wrong with selfish reasons as long as they lead you to make the ultimate commitment to the team. And if a player doesn't have that commitment, it is obvious to the players who do, and I guess we would rather have him be honest about what he wants than fake some kind of rah-rah attitude."

The idea that anyone at the highest level of a team sport would be brazen enough to voice something that contradicts all of our society's precious ideals about team play, just because it happens to be *true* . . . it will shock most of us.

Rivers laughs at the surprise. "If you're an athlete, you have to get used to it," he says. "You've got to recognize that this isn't the fantasy land we've all invented as some kind of representation of what 'real life' ought to be. Pro basketball is not real life in any way; it's not the real world. It's a bunch of incredibly competitive men playing a basically artificial game in bright-colored uniforms for very high pay in front of millions of people, most of whom don't have much idea what's going on. Most of the men who are playing it have been pampered since they were in grade school; people have given them everything, pushed them along without making them complete the steps most people have to finish, bent the rules—and now all they have to do to be big shots is dribble a ball and shoot it well. Well, most of us know it's not real life. Most of us accept it as a special job, and we decide we are going to work as hard as we can at it for as long as it is our job, but we don't do what the fans do—we don't buy the whole analogy business. Some guys do, though. Sometimes we let the praise, the easy ride, the stardom, the calls from national leaders acting all nervous in our presence, the money, we let it convince us we're doing something really grand. This has happened to me. But something usually brings me back to reality pretty fast."

Rivers laughs again. "Look, I'm a professional ballplayer. I *play ball*. I know exactly what that means—I know it's not the same as being a cancer research scientist or a schoolteacher. I don't need any illusions about being important. Basketball is not nuclear physics. But I also have nothing to apologize for—not everyone is going to cure cancer. Not everyone is going to play ball, either. As much time as that doctor put into medical school and his research, I have put into basketball. The courts have been my classroom and my office and my laboratory, and I have worked as hard as he has. Unfortunately for me, my job isn't going to last as long as his. It isn't going to help as many people, either. But if I am going to play ball, if that is going to be my work for right now, then I am going to commit myself to doing all the things, all the *basketball* things, that make me good at it."

And obviously those are the things that players need to take seriously—the perception on a given night that an opponent is favoring a tender knee and thus probably won't choose to make certain cuts in certain situations, or that one's own shooting eye is especially acute from a certain range, or that opposing teammates seem to be bickering and blaming each other as they fall behind by four in the third quarter, which means they won't be able to pull together if the lead reaches seven in the fourth, and so on. These are the signs and mechanicals of the job. Treat them trivially and you lose. But, as Rivers seems to be saying, once you have won, don't overextend the seriousness: Don't imagine you have done more than win a basketball game. This is difficult if you have millions of people saying you have just exemplified the highest qualities of the human spirit, that you are in fact an artist or a teacher or a scientist, or something even greater—some kind of genius fulfilling all sorts of American cultural ambitions we don't seem to be able to fulfill, or even express, any way but through sports. Sports played by other people.

"You have to be disciplined about it," says Rivers. "You can't begin to believe you're some kind of hero. For one thing, it will break your concentration on the games you have to play moment by moment. For another, it will make you act like a fool sometimes. And most important, if you believe the praise, you're obligated to believe the condemnation, which is sure to follow the praise as soon as you lose. If you say, 'Gee, I'm a god' when you win, you're going to have to say, 'Gee, I'm scum' when you lose. No one should ever allow himself to be tricked into thinking that badly of himself just because his team lost a basketball game, even if he himself was responsible. It helps if you know you tried as hard as you could. It's a cliché, but it's true. If you gave it your best, it doesn't hurt any less when you lose, but at least you know you deserve respect, not scorn, at least from yourself."

Rivers says that as your success increases people try to tell you what you *can't* do. "It's strange, but the more you show you're good at doing things, the more others try to fence you in. They want to talk you out of your goals and into *their* goals. But you can't let anyone talk you out of what you are after."

Fans dream the game, and expect the players to deliver the dream. If the players do, the fans deify them. If they do not, the fans treat them as something less than human. Rivers is grateful for the interest of fans, but he draws a line. He doesn't want the adulation, so he doesn't feel he has to take the crap, either.

"I love fans, and I enjoy seeing their commitment and passion. If I am out somewhere with a really recognizable star, say Dominique or Michael Jordan, and a fan walks by, I really like observing the enthusiasm and pleasure the fan gets out of seeing his idol. But I am not the fans' property. This idea, that when I am doing my job I don't belong to myself," he says, getting incredulous and stern at the same time, "this idea that I 'belong' to the fans, that a guy who pays for a ticket is my owner, with the right to pass judgment on me *and* express that judgment in terms that no decent human being would ever use toward another human being—well, it's ridiculous. You hear it all the time now—it's one of the favorite lines of the big-time sports media guys: 'Let's not forget that the fans are the real owners,' blah blah blah, 'Let's remember the guy who buys the ticket gets to call the shots,' and all that stuff."

He shakes his head in disbelief. "Do you know what this says about the importance of money over decency? What it says about the idea of 'owning'? Look—if I go into a McDonald's and I buy a hamburger and I don't like it, is it completely all right for me to trash the place, and call the manager out in front of his family and friends and tell him he's a worthless bleeping bleep bleep? How about if it's a fine French restaurant downtown? Won't I be arrested? Well, somehow we've allowed sports arenas to be places people can feel righteous behaving in ways that would get them arrested anywhere else."

Rivers mentions the famous incident a few years ago in which Charles Barkley spit at a profane heckler and hit a little girl sitting beside the guy in the stands. Barkley was universally vilified for his foulness. Spitting on a little girl! The very idea!

"But nobody ever said *anything* about the heckler," Rivers fumes. "Here was a grown man sitting beside this same little girl and screaming the foulest curses he could think of *for an entire game*. Screaming! Barkley remembered a lot of what the guy said— and it was awful stuff, all the sexual words and racial words and the whole show, insulting Barkley's family, calling him animal names, and everything. For a couple of *hours*, with this same darling little sweet girl sitting right there. But Barkley is the villain because he accidentally hit her with a mouthful of water. Barkley *was* wrong— he shouldn't have lost his temper. But wasn't the heckler just as bad? Or even worse?"

Rivers knows the aftermath of the story too. "Barkley sought out the little girl and apologized, of course. He made sure the two of them made friends with each other. This year, a bunch of us had a roast for Charles, and through his foundation we brought the little girl to speak at the roast. You know what she said? She said, 'The best thing that ever happened to me was getting spit on by Charles.' Did the heckler ever call her up and apologize for what he did in front of her? Well—who is worse?"

Worried that he sounds cranky—which he does not—Rivers calmly explains. "I'm not pointing these things out simply because I want to escape the disapproval. It's about more even than my comfort. I just feel it's bad for our society *ever* to make it acceptable for one person to treat others that way. To come up to an athlete in a restaurant, where he is eating with his wife and kids, and say, 'You suck, you bum! You guys choked!' If I reply by saying, *calmly*, 'You're wrong. We lost, but we didn't choke. We played hard,' the guy is outraged! Am I supposed to sit quietly and take his abuse, in front of my wife, just because this person paid twenty bucks for a ticket one night in February?"

His eyes burn. "It should never be okay to forget that the person you are dealing with *is* a person. I like fans, they make playing this game even more fun; but they are not entitled to so much negativity. So much resentment when we fail to fulfill them. Just because fans want to make us into something different doesn't mean we *are* something different. That's what I would like to call the fans' attention to: We are human beings. That when you call us scum, it hurts. And we are not necessarily supposed to hurt to earn our salary; we are just supposed to play basketball for our salary."

Spending twenty bucks automatically exonerates the fan from charges of being a jerk; earning two million bucks automatically turns the ballplayer into one. Forgotten in this reasoning are quite a few American principles and parallels.

"Ballplayers earn a living, a good living, by playing ball on the court," Rivers says, "but if you want to classify our work in American society, then probably you should say we are entertainers. Sports is closer to the entertainment industry than it is to anything else. For the person watching, it's a spectacle, a performance, like a movie or a concert. For the player, of course, it's something else, as it is for the musician or the actor. The lady playing the violin is concentrating on a task she wants to master because she loves doing it. She plays a tricky passage well, she feels great. The person listening is hearing something else, something romantic or sweet or nostalgic. The actor on the film makes himself cry for a certain effect; it is not necessarily sadness, it is technique, and it is satisfying for him to achieve it when it is needed. The person watching feels the sadness, and it warms him all up. There's a distance between what is done, and what is felt. A difference. With actors and musicians, the public is willing to accept the difference, even to pay for it. With athletic entertainment, not so. Why?"

Maybe it is for two reasons. First, there is a certainty to the outcome of the movie or concert. The whole thing has been packaged, controlled, edited—all of the elements have been carefully combined to produce an effect, and even if the effect is a surprise to the viewer it was a surprise calculated by the director or composer or conductor. It was under control. Knowing that the ending we have not yet reached was at least produced by calculation—that it is already set and waiting for us, unchangeable—is a comfort to us, at the beginning of a movie or concert. We don't have to risk as much; we want to be in good hands, and we know we are: Steven Spielberg is taking care of us, or Mstislav Rostropovich is.

Obviously, this isn't true in a sports contest. We don't know what the outcome will be. It defies packaging, editing, control. We are risking much more—or, at least, the athletes are risking much more, and we are going along for the ride. We are forced to accept complete uncertainty. We are not happy with this. Even though we choose it, we are not comfy inside a momentum that is not under anyone's control.

Second, athletes must deal with the opposition of relative achievement ("I played a good game" or even "I shot well in the third quarter") to absolute achievement ("We lost"). It is obvious that team players like Rivers have accepted the absolute judgment on their efforts ("Well, it was a *good* year, but not a great one"). But they also want a *little* slack ("We didn't choke. We lost, but we played hard"). Fans insist on the absolute: Win and you're okay, lose and you suck. No shadows here—only pure light, or pure darkness. Fabulous or horrible. Lose the game in the last two seconds, and no fan wants to relive the joy of the bucket that tied it thirty seconds earlier. This is different from a movie.

It definitely galls the public when an athlete does not seem to care all that much about grasping the victory within his reach. As Rivers says, fans cannot always perceive whether or not a guy or a team is trying as hard as possible; but when it *seems* a player is coasting, the indignation is righteous.

"I do understand one thing behind the readiness of the fan to criticize and resent athletes, especially when it seems a guy isn't being mature and responsible and hardworking," Rivers says. "Not only are we well paid, but we get all the breaks you can imagine. We don't know what the real world is like. People are willing to give us every sort of thing. Should we take advantage? Well, if so, we'd better at least be aware that this is unusual, that it won't last forever, and that accepting a gift is not the same as exercising responsibility.

"Responsibility is the key. It does not come automatically to a young man. A guy who has had people sweeping obstacles out of his way since he was eight or nine does not suddenly wake up on his twenty-first birthday knowing how to be a man. I'm certainly not saying we should feel sorry for athletes because we've been pampered. But we should be aware of the suddenness with which they are expected to learn behavior that other people develop over years and years of more realistic life. Look, let's say I am a rookie and I am told practice starts at twelve noon. In college, where I was a king, it was no problem to show up at ten after—nobody ever said anything. But here I show up at twelve ten and what happens? My coach screams at me and fines me five hundred dollars, my teammates resent me and treat me mean for a week to teach me a lesson, and I read five stories in the paper about how irresponsible I am. The fans read the stories, and they are ready for me next game, booing the bad guy. If I'm unlucky, I *never* get rid of the tag 'irresponsible, troublemaker, attitude problem.' This little thing might wreck a young guy's career!"

Rivers reiterates that he is not suggesting we all pity the ballplayers for their easy youth. "But who teaches these young men what it means to take responsibility? Are they suddenly supposed to be men because they are getting paid a lot of money? Somebody writing you a check is not the same as somebody teaching you to be responsible for earning it. Sometimes we have to realize we are not doing kids favors by doing them favors."

One more thing that fans in general envy athletes is the opportunity to achieve simple, inarguable victory. A clear-cut W isn't available to most people. There is so much ambiguity in life. Am I a good student? Do I study hard enough? Do other kids like me? Am I a good parent, or not? Am I working hard enough, or not? Am I getting old, or not? Fans see athletes and say: Geez, you guys can win and then you get to feel like complete successes! It's like God gives you a big thumbs-up! No one can argue with victory!

This is false, but you can see how fans believe it. Rivers points out that players do not define their lives absolutely by what they do on the court. In fact, they have the same ambiguities as the rest of us, about work, parenthood, aging. They resist the temptation to overemphasize what a victory means, or a loss. They see a steal for a steal, a basket for a basket, a missed free throw as a missed free throw. Once the game is over, they don't store themselves upright in refrigerators until the next one; they go home, shop for groceries, sit up all night with a coughing child.

"A player is simply a person who plays," Rivers says. "But a man is a person with a life full of duties, relationships, responsibilities. When they're not on the court, ballplayers are men. Because I have agreed to work under the public eye, I expect to be judged for how I do my job. But judged as a *player*, not as a man. I can accept people yelling at me if I don't do my job—for missing a bunch of layups, letting my man get open for a bunch of shots, or something like that, where I could work harder. If a player is lazy, he should hear about it. But sometimes the media and the fans fail to appreciate an effort that happens to fall short; sometimes they think that if you lost, you weren't trying." He laughs, without any rancor, and sighs. "Hey, you think stopping Tim Hardaway should be *easy*? Fighting Charles Barkley for rebounds? Taking a charge from Karl Malone? Look, playing in the NBA is a *challenge*. It's not supposed to be easy, for any of us—that's what makes the games great to watch, isn't it? It's what makes it *fun,* that's for sure. Not every move is going to work. Not every shot is going to drop. You have to keep trying new tricks. Let's remember baseball players: A guy who bats .300 is doing a great job, but he's making seven outs for every three hits. Sometimes the man I'm guarding is going to score on me, sometimes I'm going to stop a shot he should have made. I just hope to hold him even a little under what his team needs from him, and maybe score a little more than my team needs from me. If most of us do that, we win the game."

Moses

Moses Malone was the hardest-working player off the court—meaning in practice—and one of the hardest-working players on it," Doc says. Moses understood better than anybody how to get what he had to out of himself.

"Mo is unquestionably one of the great centers ever to play. But he was not a great leaper, and he did not have great hands—there were things he simply did not get as gifts. But I'd get to practice and Mo would have been there for an hour, and he'd be all sweaty already. (He is, by the way, a world-class sweating man, up there in Patrick Ewing's class.) He worked at his art. You'd see him on the treadmill, the bicycle . . . he'd tell me, 'Boy, you got to work on your legs, because your legs are going to carry you.' He used to kid Kevin Willis, and say, 'Boy, keep working on that upper body. Because I got better legs and a bigger butt, so I'll move you out of my way.' And he was right. Kevin learned it too.

"Moses could read where the ball was going on a rebound. He had the same attitude as Barkley, 'That is *my* ball, so *get* out of my way.' He was nice about it, where Barkley is mean—though they are both nice guys off court—but the message was clear: *The ball belongs to me.*

"When he was traded to the Hawks, I didn't know what to expect. I was almost fearful. I had heard he was mean and dumb and sulky, all that stuff. What a surprise! Mo was probably the funniest person I ever played with, always laughing, always talking. You looked forward to getting on the bus during those days with Moses. Really! On the bus we had a set pattern in this one section, it was like assigned seating—Spud Webb and I sat together, Nique right behind us, Randy Wittman right in front of us, Moses on the other side even with us, John Battle behind him, and Kevin in front of him. After every game, that was the way. It was funny—some guy with a ten-day contract would unknowingly get into one of these seats and we would say, 'Moses, tell the man about his seat,' and Mo would say, 'Boy, get the *hell* out of the man's seat!' Anyway—we all just looked forward to Moses opening his mouth. Moses didn't speak clearly, and he used a lot of slang; sometimes you couldn't understand what he was saying. But he would say, 'You got to *listen* better!' He had a kid's sense of enjoying life. But when the media came around, he was a different person.

"Moses was a leader. He didn't want to step on anybody's toes—when he came to the Hawks, he made a point of saying he just wanted to help the team—but he commanded respect. He's got mine. If I were coaching, I would want him on my staff somewhere. He can teach. Ask Hakeem—he'll tell you Moses taught him how to play basketball. Anyone who can teach Hakeem to play as well as he plays is someone I want teaching *my* players."

The Extra Step

I have one key strategy on defense," says Doc. "I learned it from Hank Raymonds, my coach at Marquette. He always said a simple thing: 'Get the offensive players to do one thing more than they want to do.'

"What he meant was simple: When the man you are guarding has the ball, get him to take one more (or one less) dribble than he wants to, or get him to go one foot farther to the side than he wants to, or to wait a few seconds longer than he wants to before he makes his pass. If your man doesn't have the ball, meet him a couple of feet farther out than he expects you to, make him stop and turn earlier than he wants, make him set up one foot farther out from the spot he *thought* he was going to reach quickly and easily. If he is going to catch a pass, make him take one step more than he wants toward the passer to get it.

"These are small disruptions. But they are critical. Halfcourt offensive basketball is played in a certain space, and five guys trying to coordinate a play count on having each other in the right spots within that space. If you get your guy to pick up his dribble one bounce early, and one of your teammates forces the man who was going to receive his pass one step farther out, and another teammate forces a guy who was supposed to set a pick one step off to the side, then the whole play is messed up. The passer can't throw the pass he practiced all week, the guy receiving it is not in the place he received it in all week at practice, and the guy coming to set the pick has to take longer to get there. It can really disrupt an offense. The thing is, because you are not *completely* disrupting them—remember, only a step off here and there—they will try to run the play anyway, instead of dropping it and improvising. That's what you want—you'd rather they forced the play under bad conditions.

"If you are covering a shooter who is moving without the ball, meet him farther out than he expects you to and make him fight for every inch of penetration as he tries to get to his spot. Make him bump you and push you and hip you and shove you. If you make it hard on him, chances are that soon he will stop fighting his way to his intended spot and will just kind of give up a little early. He'll get to a spot two foot farther away from the basket than his right spot, and he'll say to himself, 'Hell, this is good enough.' Fine. Let him set up there. Maybe not right away, but eventually you'll get to watch a lot of his shots hit the front of the rim—just a little bit short, because he's just that much farther out than he wants to be."

Dr. J

I was nicknamed 'Doc' because I wore a 'Doctor J' T-shirt to a clinic, but I had never met Julius Erving until the very first game I started as a pro. I was pretty nervous about it. Not because I was in awe of him, but because I wanted to *beat* him and I knew I was supposed to revere the guy. I wanted to dunk on him, I wanted to steal the ball from him, I wanted my team to win. Of course I respected him, but I didn't have room for any respect at the moment. It was time to play.

"So there we are and Doctor J walks up to me with a big smile and a handshake and says, 'Hey, Doc, what's going on?' all friendly. It made me feel like a million because he recognized me—he called *me* Doc! I didn't know what to say, so I didn't say anything. I was too tied up to talk; just shook his hand. I don't know what he thought—maybe he thought I was a jerk for not responding. But I was just kind of dazed by his easygoing manner.

"Anyway, the game starts. I was feeling pretty hot—one time I even drove down the lane and dunked on Moses. But then on one break, I'm the man back with Dr. J coming at me and Mo Cheeks on the other side, a two-on-one. Erving has the ball. And all of a sudden I am the most confused, scared rookie in the world. Because in those few seconds my mind is flashing on all the things Dr. J can do to trick me. I have seen this guy's moves and I have heard older players tell me about them—like, Billy Paultz had just told me, 'Never follow the ball with your eyes because he has huge hands and can make a move with the ball then draw it back and fool you'—and my mind about blows. I'm even thinking about how horrible it would be to injure him, how I have to be careful not to undercut him if he goes up because everybody would hate the guy who hurt the game's favorite player . . .

"Well, of course the last thing you can do if you are thinking so much is play D on a guy. So the Doctor passes off and I am so messed up concentrating on him that Cheeks takes it right in for an uncontested layup. There were just too many options. I was glad the play was over.

"Julius Erving changed the whole game. He made dunking popular—took up where Connie Hawkins left off. He made everybody notice *leaping*. He invented moves. And he made it very popular for a player to have true class. Not fake class, not just something on the surface, because of cool clothes or a slick manner, but a quality that went deep. On the court he was incredibly competitive and mean. But he was a gentleman, nobody nicer.

"He was also good at demanding that you not put him on a pedestal. He would say, 'I make mistakes. I have done many things a champion should not do. I admit and accept them, but they are still wrong. So don't go pretending I am perfect.' I love the man."

Loss

*F*or most of us, there's always something we can find to soften the smack of an apparent failure. We don't get an A in algebra, but we did come up from a C+ to a B. A salesman doesn't reach his quota this quarter, but he does improve on the sales from last year for the same period. A sixth-grade teacher sees her students' test scores fall in math, but notes that she has thirty percent more kids from remedial programs in her class this year. Success can emerge from failure, through interpretation.

Obviously, a professional athlete doesn't have the luxury of interpretation. He wins or he loses, and that's it. Ingenious argument cannot turn an L into a W. If the athlete plays for a team, he has company to share the blame or elation; if he plays for a *decent* team, he can usually count on a victory around the corner, to take away the bitterness of a recent defeat. In the long regular seasons of baseball, basketball, and hockey, there is a lot of opportunity for this sort of psyche-saving reversal. Tuesday's loss is erased by Thursday's win, and Saturday's game is just ahead. . . .

But what about the athlete who cannot be satisfied by anything but a championship? For him, a decent regular season means nothing. Individual attainments mean nothing. Everything, in fact, means nothing—only the final victory will do. That alone will make him feel a winner. Isn't this the ultimate setup for a bad fall?

100

"Sure it is," says Doc. "When you want only the thing that is the hardest to get, then you are refusing a lot of less critical satisfactions. You are almost asking for pain, because the odds are against you, huge odds. It would be stupid, if it were a conscious decision. But obsession with winning the championship isn't something you decide to feel. It just takes over. One day you realize nothing else is worth pursuing anymore—and you realize you will do anything to get to the final goal."

It is usually a veteran's goal. All the great stars gravitate toward it with an increasingly grim determination; many reach the rather drastic point of saying their stellar careers mean nothing without the big ring. In a sense this becomes true. What most of us remember and repeat endlessly about Ernie Banks and Rod Carew is that their absence from the World Series was a tragedy. Five hundred and twelve homers for Banks, seven batting titles for Carew, and all we can talk is tragedy?

Sure. How relieved were we when Dave Winfield finally got his championship? Or Elvin Hayes, or Walter Payton? It is a relief because we want to think of these great players as being complete—and we have fallen into the habit of thinking they can't quite cut it until they have acquired the championship. We feel an unmistakable pressure. Every time we watch a wonderful player who *has* won it fairly early—a Kirby Puckett, a Magic Johnson, an Art Monk, a Cal Ripken—we enjoy the fact that this pressure is already off. And when we watch marvelous veterans who haven't yet gotten there—Patrick Ewing, Don Mattingly, Steve Yzerman and Hakeem Olajuwon and Lee Smith and Charles Barkley—we want to shout, "Hurry up so we can *really* respect you!"

So—if the fans feel this way, imagine what the athletes themselves feel.

"It's not necessarily pleasant all the time, being obsessed with winning the title," says Rivers. "But it does feel *right*. What is more respectable to pursue? What expresses better the dedication to team play? The dedication to competition? This is all there is. I

101

can't even admit that I might not get it, but for the moment let's move a few years into the future and say I am looking back at my career and I did *not* win the championship. Will I feel like I wasted my life? Of course not. Will I feel like a failure? Absolutely not. But I am making these attitudes up, I am stepping way back and assuming I will have the sense to enjoy other satisfactions in retrospect. The truth is, right now I don't *want* to be satisfied by anything else. I want my team to win it all. *This* team—Patrick and Ro and Starks and Hubert and Herb and every single guy on the Knicks."

But—if you don't win it, there is that pain. And the pain is no paltry thing; it is all the worse for its absolute negativity. *We lost* is hard to say, when the only goal you define your work by is winning.

The 1992–93 Knicks believed they would win. They felt that way from the beginning: They could get the title. Not many NBA experts agreed with them. They were not the favorites, by any means—no team with eight new players could be expected to mesh the way twelve players must, to win the NBA title. Chicago, mesh-conscious, had kept its core players; Phoenix had added the willful, charismatic, incredibly talented Barkley, who would go on to surprise nobody by winning the MVP award. The Knicks had pushed the Bulls to seven games in the previous year's conference semifinals, but then the Knicks dismantled themselves. Patrick Ewing was practically a nucleus all by himself, but not quite—and, except for Charles Oakley, the only Knicks who had been retained around him were, to say the least, unproven: Greg Anthony, John Starks, Anthony Mason. The team imported Herb Williams, an old backup center; a talented enigma, Charles Smith; and a couple of aging guards, Rolando Blackman and Rivers. Bo Kimble had averaged thirty-five points as a college senior and three as a second-year pro in L.A.; maybe he qualified as an enigma too. In any case, he was functionally a rookie, along with Eric Anderson and Hubert Davis. Does this sound like a finely tuned championship machine?

"I don't care what it sounds like," says Rivers. "The feeling was there—the commitment, the chemistry, the complementary talents. Plus—we had Pat Riley in charge. Never discount the effect of Pat Riley. Those of us who were hungry could sense it. And as the season went on, despite the ups and downs in scoring, despite the injury to Ro, we got more and more certain. We could win it. This could be the year, no matter what anyone predicted."

The facts back Rivers up. The Knicks won sixty regular season games, best in the Eastern Conference, second in the NBA to Phoenix. Any team that does that has to be considered a contender. Then, in beating the Pacers and Hornets in the play-offs and splitting the first four games with the Bulls, the Knicks looked indomitable on their home court.

But then came Game Five. On their home court, the unthinkable happened. The Knicks missed fifteen free throws, Charles Smith dinked three layups in the last five seconds, and the sloppy Bulls played just exactly well enough to win by a single point.

There went the championship: A couple of nights later the Bulls won another sloppy game in Chicago to eliminate Rivers and company, then went on to maul the Suns for the title.

There is no doubt in Rivers's mind that the winner of Game Five was practically assured of winning the championship. Phoenix had little chance against either Chicago or New York, he feels; and Chicago would never have been able to beat the Knicks at home in a seventh game. One game, on your home floor, with your opponent playing poorly. But it did not work out.

"I can talk about it now," said Rivers quietly, in early September. "For the past three months, I couldn't. It hurt too much. I still had trouble accepting that we lost that game. People who were watching it on television tell me the camera caught me just after the buzzer, staring glassy-eyed and walking slowly off the court. They say I looked like I had died. Well . . ."

Rivers says the hardest thing about losing the game—and with it the championship, in effect—was the apparent impossibility of it. "We just *could not lose*," he says, still shaking his head incredulously. "It simply never occurred to us. We had set out to do something, we had worked harder than anyone, we had almost gotten to the goal, things seemed to be going our way—and then it was reversed. How did it happen? It felt like the sudden death of a family member who was perfectly healthy. I'm not saying that losing a basketball game is as bad as someone dropping dead, of course—but I am accurately describing the *feeling*. One so shocking that it really could not be believed. We walked off the court, we sat around the locker room, we talked to the press, we showered and dressed, but there was no reality to it. I remember a lot of microphones in my face, and I remember having just enough presence of mind to say something about being ready to win Game Six in Chicago, but I don't recall much more from right after the game."

Eventually Rivers got in his car for the drive home to Connecticut. In the car, he fumed and fidgeted. Outside the city, heading north on the dark highway at about two in the morning, Rivers felt he had to pull over and get out for some air. He stopped at a gas station. One other car was there, and its owner was standing over the pumping nozzle in the rear of his vehicle with his head in both hands. It was a scene from some bleak nocturnal science-fiction movie. And the man with his head in his hands was Herb Williams.

Rivers drove on. He saw almost no other cars until he spotted a police cruiser up ahead on the right shoulder with its lights flashing. As he approached, he noticed another car pulled over, with its driver now standing outside, showing identification to the cop. The driver was Charles Smith.

"What next?" Rivers thought. "Bad night for Knicks. Just let me get home."

Before he went to bed, he knew what he needed: to play ball. He needed to get to Game Six, for some relief, some action, the chance to *do* something. The sooner he went out and met the next game coming, the better he would feel. So the following day, he went into the city early and hit the gym, to shoot around. "We had an afternoon flight to Chicago," he said, "but I was out on the court around ten. Just shooting. After a while Herb Williams came, and went down to the other end, and the two of us just shot and shot and shot, silently. Then Herb came up to my end, and we shot, still silent. Finally, one of us said something about the game. And we stood there for half an hour, talking about it, holding the balls.

"Patrick showed up to shoot too. He had a trainer rebound for him, and he just stood down at the other basket firing up long jump shots. Nobody else came out, but all the players eventually stopped in, to pick up their gym shoes and stuff. They'd peek out and see us shooting, then shake their heads and duck back. Herb and I were just working out the hurt, but Patrick was there with a purpose. He was sending a message to the other players that there was no time for sulking: We had to get ready for the next game. He was down there sweating and *practicing*. Everybody got the message. You can't help but get the message when Patrick sends it. He is an incredible leader, and he knew this was a moment to step up and show the way."

The Knicks were professional enough, and confident enough, that by the time Game Six came, they believed they could win it and send the series back to New York. "I wouldn't have played if I didn't believe we would win," Rivers says. "We all came around to feel that way—we went out on the floor ready to win. But I can't pretend we felt quite the same as we did before Game Five, when it was *impossible* to consider losing."

He sighs. "So then we lost, and it was over. We flew back to New York right after the game. I got home sometime before dawn, and Kris came down and gave me a hug and went back upstairs. She knew I wasn't going to bed anytime soon. I sat in a chair and watched some stupid movie and didn't see a thing. Then, just at dawn, this family of geese—I had never seen anything like this before—these geese from a pond down the road came walking right up my driveway and under my window, the mother and the father and the little fuzzy babies. Just like they had come to pay their respects. Next thing I knew, the kids were up, and they came down and it was a new day, no problem, 'Hi, Daddy!' But they knew. Jeremiah knew what had happened, and they could all feel something dark around me. One of their friends came over, and she heard we had lost, so she came up to me, all bright and cheerful, and said, 'It's great you lost!' I asked her why, and she said, 'Because now you can be on vacation!' "

He laughs. "Her mother called me later, horrified. 'I'm so sorry about what Samantha said!' I told her it was no problem—Samantha was actually right. She was just giving me the kids' reality: Vacation is where it's at. But for an athlete chasing a championship, you never want a vacation."

The vacation came, however unwanted, and now it is almost over: Training camp starts in a month. Rivers cannot wait.

"Losing last year hurt more than we could imagine, but getting to that point was full of pain too. We had to work *so* hard all year, and push through injuries, and push through limits we had accepted in ourselves," he says. "So now here we are back at the beginning all over again with nothing to show for all that suffering and disappointment. And you know what? We would all gladly go through *ten times* the pain if it could get us to the championship. *Gladly.* Because we learned last year that we could hurt and survive. We learned we could suffer more than we thought possible and come out standing. So we are ready again. Whatever it takes, we know we can do it. *That's* the lesson. That's what's going to make us better. We know we can take anything and go past the limits."

Rivers smiles excitedly. He obviously *is* eager for the whole thing to start again; he can't wait to get together with the other eleven guys and commence the long, painful trek. Getting shot down has not made him gun-shy; it has made him look for a bigger gun—and he feels the Knicks have upped their caliber by learning these hard lessons and staying together. He rattles off something about each teammate. Charles learned a lot from his first year of being a role player on a good team, instead of being the hotshot on bad ones; Greg is ready to break through and become the star point guard he is supposed to be; Starks will work harder and get better as he resists the distractions of sudden fame; Ro is healthy, Herb signed a new contract, Hubert showed a lot of guts in the play-offs, Patrick will be Patrick again but more so, etc., etc., etc. After ten minutes he is bouncing off the walls, looking around for a basketball and a hoop and a teammate to pass to.

"Man, I love this," he says unnecessarily. His eyes spark with enjoyment and anticipation, but there is a cold meanness there too. "We are going to get *after* it."

His smile turns grim. "Pat Riley has a saying: *Humiliation before honor.* We've paid some dues, and we'll pay some more. Bring on whatever your idea of humiliation is, and we'll work our way right through. We are ready. For some honor. For the only honor that still counts."

Dad

*I*n almost all the stories of a boy's rise to sports stardom, there is a handsome, Kodak-commercial role for the father. Usually he is the First Teacher, patiently lobbing rubber balls underhand to the four-year-old who will grow up to be Dave Justice or Chuck Knoblauch. Or he is the Sage Counselor, gruffly hugging the mud-speckled little halfback who fumbled away the Pee Wee championship, assuring the future Barry Sanders that this mistake is a great opportunity to learn about holding on to the ball. Or perhaps, as seems to happen more and more, Dad is himself a big-leaguer, and Junior's storybook ascent seems a magical matter of genes, plus boyish adulation that turns into a young man's personal quest. We have Ken Griffey and Ken Griffey Jr., Dolph Schayes and Danny Schayes, Rick Barry and Jon Barry, Bob Boone and Bret Boone (*and* Bret's grandfather, too), Diego Segui and David Segui, Mel Stottlemyre and Todd Stottlemyre, Cesar Cedeño and Andujar Cedeño, Terry Metcalf and Eric Metcalf . . .

Of course, the only pop-and-kid ball-playing combo in which both could be called true stars is: Bobby and Barry Bonds. Barry, however, robbed us early on of the chance to wax sentimental about his lineage by confessing frankly that he resented his father awfully—for being away from home so much, for never coming to Barry's games, for not just being a normal everyday presence. A few years later Barry added that he had learned enough from living the ballplayer's life himself that he was now ready to forgive Bobby. But it is not the classic story of A Jock and His Boy.

Doc Rivers's dad was not a ballplayer; he was a policeman in Maywood, the Chicago suburb that is Doc's hometown. His relationship to his son's career, and indeed to his son himself, does not exemplify any of the classic roles. In fact, the whole thing sounds pretty odd when Rivers describes it—most odd, perhaps, in the way it cuts through the usual mannerisms of father and son and deals with the essentials in bald honesty.

"My dad was home a lot, but he was not home a lot too," Rivers says. "He has always been his own man. He does what he needs to do, without seeming to care a bit for what the rest of us might feel he is *supposed* to do. For example, it is not unusual for him to be gone when Kris and I arrange to go home for a visit, with the kids and all. We'll show up, Dad won't be there, I'll ask Mom, 'Where's Dad?' and she'll just say, 'He went fishing.' That's it. No point in inquiring further. This summer he was there for four days, and it was great—only the second time he has seen Austin. About the fourth time he has seen Callie—and she's four years old. When I was growing up, it was kind of like that too; you never knew just when he would be there. But—and this is the key thing—somehow he managed to be a good father. He fulfilled his responsibilities. He was the strong presence. It was just hard to figure out exactly *how*."

One conventional thing his father *did* do, says Rivers, is come to his son's basketball games. All through high school, and even into college and the first year or two of the NBA, his father came to games. "I could count on that," Rivers says. "My mom, and my dad, at the games."

But then, all of a sudden, his father stopped coming entirely. "Just never showed anymore." Rivers shrugs. "Never! I would always leave tickets, Mom would always come, but no Dad. I asked her about it, and she said he once just said, 'Oh, Glenn's all right,' and that was the end of it. Okay, but frankly it bothered the hell out of me. It *still* bothers me in a way. Sometimes he would call—for example, after Game One against Chicago last year I picked up the phone, and his voice came over the line: 'Get more aggressive!' That was all—no 'Hi, Glenn,' or anything. Just a tip—or, I should say, a command! It was like that growing up, too. I'd play a great game, and wait for him to say something, *anything*, like 'Good game, Son!' you know. I'd wait for a little applause. But on the rare occasions when he said anything, he'd just say, 'Yeah, well, you missed two free throws in the fourth quarter' . . ."

Rivers shakes his head. "But I'll tell you something. There are people in your life who are always around, who are there *all* the time—except for the few key moments when you really need them. There are *lots* of these people. Then—much more rare—there are people who are never there *except* when you absolutely need them. That's my dad. He would disappear, but when I needed him, when I *had* to have him, throughout my life, he was there. He never missed. He knew. And that's why he showed up last year for the last game against the Bulls, the game when we lost it all."

Rivers says his father had not come to a game of his own accord for six or seven years. Doc left tickets, and his mother brought other people. He was used to it. But before Game Six, he had the premonition of need. "I asked my mom, 'Is Dad coming?' It wasn't like there was any expectation or anything, of course, after six or seven years of no-show. She said, 'Glenn, I don't know, and I'm certainly not going to *ask* him.' You didn't ask my father such things—you left him to his own plans. So I left the tickets and put it out of my mind and went out and played. And we lost. A few minutes later, as we're all sitting there in shock and pain, the very first person to bust into the locker room is—my dad."

Rivers was trying gamely to make a proud speech to the reporters assembled around him—the standard but sincere "We fought hard but it wasn't enough" sort of speech—and he saw his father standing against the wall, waiting until the press left his boy alone.

"His eyes were red," Rivers said. "He had been crying. Because he knew I was hurting. That alone almost made me cry; later, in fact, it did. But I was talking to the reporters and I had to stay composed. My father was not only sad, though—he was *mad*. I could see he wanted to wade into those reporters and fling 'em all away and grab me and put me on a bus home and say, 'Go home. Relax. It's finished.' He knew what I needed. Later he told me: 'I am glad it's over. Your body has had enough for now.' He put my personal condition, my most fundamental need—good health— first. The hell with the championship: He knew I was coming apart at the seams and he wanted me to rest."

Rivers sighs. "I didn't want to rest. I wanted to play until we won. But the fact that he could see it the way he did meant he was thinking like a father. He was *always* thinking like a father, even when you couldn't know he was. That's why he was there, for that one game, for the first time in years."

Rivers thinks. "I guess the message my father sends by staying away is: 'You're okay. You don't need me.' It's a way of calling attention to what he knows about me, what he knows about my strength. He's a very confident man, very secure. He's trying to make me realize I am secure too. It's a tough kind of technique. It's a sort of realistic attitude you don't see a lot. But what makes it work is the fact that he also recognizes those times when I *do* need somebody else. When I need *him*. And I know he will always be there. Always. He will never miss. He'll know."

Rivers smiles. "I can live with that. What more can you ask of anyone, really?"

J-Man's Dad

*J*eremiah Rivers, age five, is pouring Rice Krispies into his bowl before going off to camp for the day. "Daddy," he says.

Glenn Rivers, age thirty-two, is shaking Frosted Flakes into *his* bowl. "Yes, J-Man?"

"Is it bragging to tell someone my dad is Doc Rivers?"

Doc Rivers pours milk onto Jeremiah's cereal. "No, Jeremiah. It's not bragging."

"Are you sure?"

"Yes." They both eat a bite.

"Why isn't it bragging, Daddy?" says Jeremiah, chewing.

Doc waits until he has swallowed his Frosted Flakes. "Because I *am* your daddy. You're just saying so. But mostly because it's no big deal that your daddy is Doc Rivers."

"Oh."

"Your daddy is mainly your daddy."

"Oh."

"You want some more cereal?"

Jeremiah holds up his bowl. Doc pours. Then he says, "You know what I tell people?"

"What?"

"I tell people, 'My son is Jeremiah Rivers.' "

"You do?"

"Yes, I do. And they say, 'He *is*?' They say, 'That *good* boy, he's your son?' And I say, 'That's right.' They say, 'We know about him. You are a lucky man.' And I say, 'I sure am.' Now you tell me, J-Man," says Doc, pouring a little more milk on the Rice Krispies, "is that bragging?"

"No, Daddy. It's okay."

"That's what I think," says Doc. "I think it's *very* good."

Johnny Davis

When I was a rookie in Atlanta," Doc says, "I was behind the veteran point guard Johnny Davis. Johnny had been in the league for about ten years, and it was obvious what the situation was: I was the young kid who was trying to take his job.

"He was the starter for the first few games. The team had a slow start. Then Johnny got injured, and I took his place. The team turned it around and ran off a good streak. Then Johnny came back, and I went to the bench, and the team slowed down again.

"It was *not* because of Johnny that the team slipped. But to the fans and the media it was easy to say: 'Hey, with the kid Rivers in there the Hawks were hot, and with Davis they slacked off.' So a potential controversy was brewing. Before long, the coach decided to try me again, and I began to start. I wanted to start, of course; I wanted to beat Johnny out of his job, naturally. I assumed he would be resentful, and I was trying to be sensitive to his position as the old guy being overtaken by the brash kid, so I basically stayed away from him.

"Then before one game he called me over. He was very calm and straightforward. 'Do you know anything about so-and-so, who you are guarding tonight?' he asked me. I said I didn't know much about the guy. Johnny nodded, and said, 'I'll tell you what. I have a book in my head about every player you will face this year. I will give you a choice. You can sit with me, and you can listen to me, and I will tell you everything I know. Or, if you prefer—and I will respect this—you can go out and learn for yourself, and probably get burned half the time. It's up to you. You are welcome to use my experience.' "

Rivers shakes his head reverentially. "I could barely believe it. Here was the guy whose job I was taking, and he was going to help me play better. Because we were teammates and he was a team player, but also because he simply felt it was a good gift to give. He knew he could help a young player and it was the right thing to do, even if it hastened him to the bench.

"Johnny Davis made me a player far earlier than I would have become one. Some of the things he taught me I would have learned the hard way all by myself, but some of them I might never have picked up. He was a great professional; I owe him a lot. It's a debt I want to repay, happily, by helping anyone I can the same way."

Desperate

*I*n the quick, switching flow of a game, are there sudden moments when a player finds himself utterly calm, almost silent, capable of a kind of deliberation that seems impossible at the real pace of the play? I mention to Rivers two late-fourth-quarter plays from the 1993 play-offs in which he seemed to function with that kind of coolness.

One was in the fourth game against the Hornets, in Charlotte. Muggsy Bogues stole the ball, drove the length of the court incredibly fast, and threw up a wild layup that did not go—but Larry Johnson was there to dunk the rebound and tie the game. Maybe a minute remained. If Charlotte won, the series would be 2–2. Doc took the ball in and brought it upcourt patiently. But just over the halfcourt line, he picked up his dribble and two players trapped him immediately, arms waving, bodies right up against him.

What did he do? He kept his eyes open, waited for the right gap, stepped between the two torsos and four arms, and threw a perfect 1952-Celtics-style two-handed bounce pass to Charles Oakley underneath. Oakley hit the layup, was fouled by Larry Johnson, hit the free throw, and the game was essentially over.

The other play was very similar. In Game One of the series against Chicago, Rivers found himself trapped in the right corner by (gulp) Scottie Pippen and Michael Jordan. Arms waving (*long* arms), chest-to-chest pressure, twenty-four feet from the basket, clock ticking . . . but then Doc stepped through the trap, and the ball was out too, and *smap* there was another two-handed bounce pass that came up to Anthony Mason just an inch out of Horace Grant's reach, and Mason hit the layup.

How about it? Did the whole world slow down for him during these moments? Was he in some zone of cool intelligence, heart barely beating, clock barely ticking?

"Hell no!" he laughs. "I remember both of those plays completely, and I was absolutely *desperate*. I may have looked cool, but that was just the blank effect of terror. The play against Chicago—I went to the wing with the ball, there was supposed to be a pick and roll, but Patrick got held and couldn't set the pick, Scottie came over and got me, and I thought, 'I'm going to take him baseline, to the hoop.' But before I could make my move, *Jordan* jumps over! So instead of driving past Scottie, I am trapped by these monster guys. I squirm through and I look around and in my head I am screaming: *Somebody get open!* With my eyes I am shooting looks at everybody: *Please, somebody!* And I spot Mase high in the paint, and I can see Horace is a step behind him, so I *glare* at him, I mean it's like a death ray I am firing with my eyes: *Get your tail open! Come down and you're open!* He catches my look and interprets it just right and makes the move. Horace is right behind him, I have exactly one small space to get the ball through, and I pass it. Mase hits the shot. Jordan says, 'Aw, man. We had you.' "

Rivers pretends to wipe sweat off his forehead. "It was just one of those moments when your options are all eliminated. In one way, it seemed to take twenty seconds for Mason to get open. In another way, it felt like what it was—an incredibly pressured second and a half. The pass was easy, because there was only one place to put it. What's hard is the moment when you have lots of options. When there's only one play to make, you make it easily."

The look he gave Mason became a bit of team lore. "Mase said, 'Man, you looked like you were going to *kill* me!' I said, 'No,

Mase, I didn't have *time* to give you any kind of a look.' He laughed and told me we'd see when we watched the tape. So later, we were watching, the whole team, and there it was: I looked like I was going to absolutely kill him. Everybody laughed, 'Look out for Doc, he's *mean!*' But it was actually just good communication in a tight spot: Mase had to read what I wanted; he had to pay attention and be smart enough to make the right move. But *calm*? Never. There is a lot of *fear* out there. Fear is a great motivation if you use it right. You just hope your teammates help you out."

DJ

***D**ennis Johnson was clutch. He was a lot like Maurice Cheeks. What needed to be done, at the right moment, he would do. Clutch, clutch guy. A winner, everywhere he played.*

"DJ was very articulate and stood up for what he believed in. He declined to play the charm game, so he angered some reporters and they tagged him with this reputation, 'attitude problem.' That's why the Celtics got him from Phoenix.

"He was not the most talented guy—not super quick or a great shot—but he could do everything well enough to take over when a game was on the line. One thing he was superb at was defense. He played position very well, he had great reach. He's a classic example of one of Red Auerbach's ingenious insights into the game. Auerbach always got these players with tremendously long arms. He said, 'Don't measure a player's height by where his *head* reaches to: Measure it by where his *arms* reach to.' So you see him with Bill Russell, Don Chaney, Kevin McHale, Robert Parish, Cedric Maxwell, Larry Bird, Reggie Lewis, DJ—all these *long*-armed guys. It worked, too, didn't it? You don't grab rebounds with your head. You use your hands, and they're on the ends of your arms.

"He was never a good shooter, DJ—but he always hit the big shots. When we played the Celtics, especially in the play-offs, we'd give him shots all game long. But when it came down to the wire, we did *not* want him taking a shot. Same thing playing D: Because he wasn't that quick, you might be able to go around him all day. But then when the game was on the line, he'd steal it from you.

"DJ worked the refs as well as anyone could. He'd moan and cry the whole game; you'd say, 'Dang, this guy thinks he can't be touched.' But then, every now and then, he'd get a call. So it was worth it.

"All those years, the fans and everyone in the media talked about Larry, and they should have. Larry was obviously the best, and without him those teams wouldn't have won anything. But all the players in the league also talked about DJ. He was just this shadow in the background, laughing, having a great time winning. Winning it all."

The Coach

I don't know what makes a great coach," says Doc Rivers. "I do know that as in many things, there is not one way, or one style to success. Pat Riley, Chuck Daly, Phil Jackson all do it their own personal way—they are all original, and maybe that is an ingredient of success: being yourself.

"There are traits that I believe a coach must have to be a great coach for a long time, year in and year out. I emphasize the long haul, because players can be conned in the short term, but a coach who dupes players won't have a long-term success. We find out if a coach is conning us, or manipulating us, or lying to us, and when we catch on, that team is going down. An immediate nosedive. If you take a close look at teams in all sports you can see great examples of this: A team will have a big year under a new coach, maybe two—and then after half of the next year, *bang*, they flop. Obviously there are other reasons teams do this besides coaches who have lost their players' confidence, but you'd be surprised how often this is the reason."

Rivers says he believes that to be a great coach a person must attain two things: respect from the players, and trust from the players.

"Trust is the most important. The players must trust you. If they do, the respect will follow. By trust, I mean that the players must feel you believe in what you are trying to sell them. They must believe you are committed to the things you say you are committed to—there can be no hidden agendas. The players will discover the deception, maybe not right away, but soon enough. They will see right through you, and then they won't respect you and they won't work for you. They will continue to commit themselves to trying to win games, but they'll do it their own ways, and that means disorder eventually. Twelve guys trying to win twelve ways means the team loses."

Rivers says absolute honesty of commitment is what makes Pat Riley so good. "He sees himself as, simply, the coach. And the coach must be committed to one thing: winning. Not just winning games, but winning it *all*. No side items—only a championship. He wants to be the *best* coach, on the best team, just as a player wants to be the *best* player, on the best team. Players are willing to do for Riley whatever it takes to win, because they trust him. When he gives out roles on the team, you might agree or disagree with what he asks of each guy—but you are willing to do whatever he asks because you know it is for the *win*.

"Last year we worked incredible hours in practice. Frankly, I think sometimes we worked too long; certainly we griped sometimes, but we did it, we did everything Riley asked, because we *believed*. And we could see *him* working too. Even in something as meaningless as the pregame talk. I'll be honest with you—most pro players don't give a hoot for the coach's pregame talk, because most coaches never say anything you haven't heard a thousand times before, things the players already know. It's just going through the motions: The coach has to fill in the time, and the players are sitting there thinking about whatever they need to concentrate on for the game. But Coach Riley was different. After a few pregame talks, I noticed he was really *trying:* He had written some very smart speeches. His talks applied to the game ahead, they all had their own moral or purpose, they were beautifully written. You could see he was leaving no detail of his job undone—he was going to make everything count if he could, make everything contribute to the overall goal, even the five minutes most coaches kind of blow off."

Rivers says it is not true that Riley just gets respect because he won in Los Angeles or because he played for several years. "Sometimes that will get him the benefit of the doubt on a small matter, but in other cases his past experience won't count for anything with us. It doesn't matter to a player whether or not a coach played ball in the NBA: What matters is whether he can *coach* in the NBA. If he earns our trust and respect, we don't care if he ever made a single foul shot in his life. If you get our trust, we will follow you. Lose the trust, and you are on your own."

Mike Fratello was Rivers's coach for years in Atlanta, and the experience Rivers gained from watching Fratello wear out his welcome on the Hawks has taught the player a lot. "Fratello was in many ways a good coach. He had a lot of insights and ideas, and certainly he was committed. He took that team to a pretty good level of winning for several years in a row, though we couldn't get over the hump. But for whatever reason, the players began to feel he didn't trust them, and in turn they began to distrust him. Respect, too—the players felt Mike didn't respect them as well as he could. Mike was a yeller and screamer, and that kind of coach usually gets some performance out of most players, but after a point they just tune him out; they don't believe in the intensity anymore. All that high-pitched noise doesn't give him any space to raise his voice any higher when he needs to. I remember Moses Malone saying once to him, on the sideline during a game when Mike was yelling at him: 'Mike, what you are saying is probably right. But there's a better way to tell me. I've got three kids sitting up there in the stands, watching you yell at me. I'm a man, Mike. Treat me like one.' At the time I thought, 'Dang, I got two kids up there myself. Mo is right.' To his credit Fratello realized he was doing it wrong, and he changed. He really tried to correct himself. But by the time he changed, it was too late—he had lost the trust of that particular team. Mike's methods were sometimes wrong, I thought when I played for him. But I realize now he wanted us to win. That experience has helped me as a player. And it will help Mike in Cleveland. I think he will be better the second time around. I think this time he will see that respect has to flow both ways."

Nique

Dominique Wilkins is one of those players who actually *are* 'naturals'—in his case, the cliché about 'pure athletic ability' fits. Nique never worked out much, never played in the summer, never practiced extremely hard. But he had a huge drive for competition, a drive to be the best. And to be *recognized* as one of the best. In fact, that's something I feel hurt him as a player. He needed to have that acknowledgment, he wanted so badly to be included in that Magic-Michael-Bird category that he thought about it, let it eat at him at times when he could have just been concentrating on *his* game and letting it speak for himself. Frankly, I always thought all Nique needed to do was play, and if he did so, the recognition would come even if he didn't go out to meet it. I think he has realized this now, and he has been a better player the last couple of years.

"It's amazing. Here's a guy who didn't work out much, but come game time he had that rare energy level of a Michael Jordan. Nique came to play every night. You hear people say he didn't, but they don't know what they are talking about. Dominique was ready to do it in every game, and he worked *hard* on the court. He could be sick, he could be tired, the rest of the team could be off, he could have Larry Bird all over him, but Nique was going to give you twenty-eight points and ten rebounds and that was what you got. He was a great guy to play with.

"Nique did not understand the game. He was not a student of the game—he was not 'educated' in the game. He just didn't look at basketball that way. Nique played on pure instinct and pure athleticism. He did begin to learn as he went on, and by now he has come to understand a lot. I believe right now he may be at his best. But the trouble is, he is just at that point where he knows a lot, knows what to do, but his body is beginning to hold him back. So this past summer he worked out every day, for the first time. And he recognized that it was good for you.

"Nique is certainly one of the best players I have ever played with, but he is not a leader. It's not in his personality. He doesn't want to be the leader, he doesn't know how to do it, he is uncomfortable trying to do it. That has hurt him and his team. He is by far the best player on his team, but he is not the leader. And anytime you have that situation, you have a problem. Your best player must be your leader. Otherwise, a lesser player has to take charge, but that player can be usurped of his authority at any time by the better guy, whether the better guy intends to take it away or not. The reason is simple: Players follow the best *player*. Whether he leads or not. If the player *is* a leader—Patrick Ewing, Michael Jordan, Magic, Bird, Isiah—then you have a good situation.

"Not being a leader is the only negative thing about Nique. He is always called a ball hog, but it isn't true. Nique is not a selfish player, not at all. Nique was taught that to win, you score. He played that way because he thought that was his best contribution to the team. It was. There is nobody better at it. The only thing that hurt him, as I said, was his insecurity—his need to be reassured that he was great. People can't believe this: They can't believe a player of Dominique Wilkins's obvious talent needs to be told he's good. But he does need it—we all do, every single player. He just needed it more than most, and it robbed him. Nique and I are very good friends; I feel I know him very well, how generous a person he is, what a nice guy he is—but I have always been shocked by his need for this reassurance. One day he will realize he is at the top. The rest of us already know it."

Shots

*F*or offensive skills," says Doc, "the key is repetition. Do it and do it and do it again. Take shooting. Starting out, I was not a good shooter—I was even a poor shooter. But I became a pretty good shooter—a decent shooter, an average NBA shooter—by practicing in a simple way that Randy Wittman taught me. He was a great shooter I played with in Atlanta.

"I did the same thing every day at the end of team practice. I stood close to the basket and made a layup. Then I took one step back and I made a shot from there. Then I stepped back and made another one, and so on, all the way to the last shot in my range, which was about at the three-point line. Then I took one *more* step back. Out of my range. Out of bounds, in fact. Beyond what I was comfortable with. And I shot until I made that one there. Before too long, that last shot was *within* my range.

"Then I would go to the five or six places on the floor where I usually take shots from in a game. Everybody has these spots, and you'd better know where yours are! From each of these spots I would make five shots in a row.

"Five in a row. This sounds easy, but it can take a long time— you can be in that gym forever. Five shots in a row is a lot to make from each spot. Sometimes, when you are not hitting, you get really sick of a spot, and you want to say, 'Hey, I'll just move on to the next spot; I'll get my five from here tomorrow.' Or you'll say, 'I've gotten pretty good, so three from each spot is enough for now.' That's what happens to most guys. They let a little of the determination go, a little of the pressure off. And those are the guys you will beat, when you meet them, if you stick with your *five* in a row. The difference between a guy who is going to be good and a guy who *says* he wants to be good is that, while they both start out with the intention of hitting five, only one of them does so." Rivers holds up five fingers. "If the rule is five, hit five. Then *increase*. Never rest."

Rivers smiles. "When I was in Atlanta, after Witt had taught me to recognize my spots on the floor, I would very often find myself on one of them at a tense moment in the game, and I would be grinning inside. I would be saying, 'Hey! I make five in a row from here every day! No problem!' And *skoosh*, I'd shoot nice and easy. Nobody in the gym knew that was one of my spots; nobody knew I was habituated to hitting from there. But look: During my practice, maybe I hit three in a row and missed, then two in a row and missed, then three and missed, then finally I hit my five. Now, that is thirteen for sixteen shooting! That's a percentage anybody will take, anytime. If you've done your practice on your spots, you'll be *delighted* to take a shot with four seconds left and the game on the line. That's *your* shot."

Rivers makes the point that there are ten different ways to do anything in basketball, ten different ways to get to the final point— which, in shooting, for example, is the point where the ball goes through the hoop. "You will meet coaches who insist there is only one right way. They'll tell you, 'You have to shoot with your arm held away from your body like this,' or 'You can only shoot if your head is bent ten degrees back,' or whatever they have decreed is The Way. This is wrong. You should do everything in a way that is comfortable to you. Use a motion that is natural to you. If it keeps failing—if people keep stealing your dribble or blocking your shot—then you need to make some changes, but don't just go and completely adopt somebody else's motion. Find a motion of your own that works.

"There are some *ugly* shooters in basketball. True, there are some 'textbook' jump shots, but there are also some good shooters who break the coaches' rules of pretty shooting. Michael Adams— a hideous shot, but he's good for sixteen to eighteen points a game and he's five-ten. Jamaal Wilkes had a terrible-looking shot, but he was tremendous at *making* it. Larry Bird! Larry Bird shot a very flat ball, not much backspin. But how about it—did Larry Bird ever hit any big shots in his career?

"How many players do you see who shoot the same way? Not many. Each of us has a different set of legs and arms and eyes, and we move different ways. Yes, there are fundamentals you need to learn. Kevin McHale and I were talking about them once, and we came up with a couple: Bend your knees, and follow through. Those are probably a good idea for everyone. But if you practice a 'bad' habit enough, you can get good at it. Rick Majerus, a great coach who was an assistant at Marquette when I was there, told me that a player shoots the way he walks. For example, there is a certain way you move your arms when you walk, and that's how you will raise the ball when you take your natural shot. We all find a way to shoot that feels good. The best way to tell is to see if the ball keeps going in the basket."

Sly and Eddie

Sly Williams was a tremendously powerful and talented player. He could do everything. He had probably the best instincts I have ever seen—instincts like Jordan and Bird. A great ball-handler for a big man, and a terrific passer. A confident player. A tough player. I remember once he told off Rick Mahorn, and Mahorn didn't even lift his head to look at him. He was very enjoyable to play with.

"But he got into drugs. And we all knew it was just a matter of time before he lost everything. I tell kids about him because he illustrates the power of drugs: Here was a guy making $800,000 a year and he couldn't make do without drugs. He threw it all away for drugs.

"It was tough. As a player, you just don't know what to do when a teammate is killing himself this way. Do you help? Do you say something to the guy? Do you dare? Do you try to get close to him so he'll listen to you? If you're young, you don't want to get too close and tied up, because it's a small league and you're afraid of having everyone think you're on the same track, you have the same trouble. It's hard to decide what to do.

"I remember the Hawks trying to deal with the problem with Eddie Johnson. Fast Eddie—incredible player. We had a team meeting once without him, and we all said, 'Nobody give him any money when he asks for it!' and stuff like that, but we didn't figure out a way really to help him, or Sly. We let them down, just as they let us down. They might have been yelling for help, waiting for us to rescue them, but we didn't hear, or we didn't figure out how to respond. The team was trying, but most of us just wanted the problem to go away. This was years ago and we didn't know yet that drugs *don't* go away.

"Now I might handle it better. I would at least tell the player I knew about the drugs, and I knew he needed to get some help. The player would probably not care much, or deny it, but at least he might think about the fact that people *knew*—it could make some difference.

"Sly and Eddie are both in jail right now. I got a sad letter from Eddie. Now, Eddie and I didn't get along when we were team-mates. I was going after his job, and I was starting. He was insecure—cocaine makes you insecure, and he was that way anyway—so he despised me. He tried every little trick with me, to mess me up and get his job back. Later, we got along okay when he was sober—he was a surprisingly smart guy—but he was not sober much. So we were kind of enemies.

"But just a few weeks ago I got a letter from Eddie. From prison. It was a nice letter—'You're doing great, man, keep it up, work hard, keep pushing . . .' And then at the end he says, 'Do you have any extra shoes? Can you send me some gym shoes?' "

Rivers sighs heavily, shakes his head. "Man, here is a two-time All-Star, one of the quickest and most dangerous guards you could find, a bright guy, went to Auburn University—and he is asking me to send him some old shoes in jail."

Taking Leave

*I*n many ways the career of a pro athlete has more in common with the life of a bird than it does with the normal professional life of most humans in America. A bird's heart beats five hundred times a minute, which makes you pretty quick; everything else in the world seems to be moving kind of slowly. Birds have amazing physical capabilities that intensify their experience of the world around them: Their senses, especially vision, are outrageously acute, and of course they can fly. A bird's livelihood is so completely dependent on its high-performance physical gifts that the slightest injury can bring its whole existence to utter ruin. And, finally, for all of its intensity, a bird's life is brief.

The brevity of an athlete's career is something most of us never think about. We notice when a guy seems to have been around forever—a Dave Winfield or a Moses Malone or a Bryan Trottier—but we tend to regard such figures as the norm. After all, having a job for eighteen years doesn't really seem all that special, does it? The briefer guys—the Mark Fidryches, the Marques Johnsons—we simply forget about. It's as if they were never here.

And what about the place an athletic career occupies in the run of a man's life? Rod Langway retired last year as an absolute grandpa in the National Hockey League—he wore no helmet, his face was getting grooved and gaunt, his hair was thin, his ferocious physical strength had obviously dried up, he suffered little injuries all the time, his style of defensive play was way old-timey: Bye-bye, Rod, you grand old lion, you've earned a few years in a rocking chair.

But Rod Langway was thirty-five. Thirty-five! At an age when most professionals are just finding their feet, a jock has to consider himself washed up. His friends who are schoolteachers or accountants or masons or lawyers are moving into their prime, using seven or eight years of work experience as the basis for a steady, confident, long-term growth, but the athlete has to face the fact that he is on the way down and out. And there is nothing gradual about his decline: In most pro careers, when things start to go, they go fast.

A man often defines himself largely by his ability to work. His self-esteem, his sense of responsibility fulfilled, his deepest personal satisfactions, intimately reflect how well he does his job. A player in the NBA or NHL or NFL or major league baseball gets the opportunity to think very highly of himself at an unusually young age: He's at the top of his field in his mid-twenties. But this chance for self-respect comes too early for most players; twenty-four-year-olds rarely worry much about self-esteem and personal duty. And by the time of life when most men *are* looking for such reassurances of their self-worth, the athlete must instead contend with the conclusion that he is worthless at his work. Worthless, in his mid-thirties, when he has a wife who is entering *her* prime and two kids under seven.

Another weird aspect of an athlete's decline is the inverse relationship between experience and value. In most fields, the passage of years increases a man's value: Experience brings wisdom. It brings wisdom in sports, too, but the wisdom isn't worth a hoot unless the legs and eyes and hands can deliver the goods. Rod Langway and Larry Bird and Nolan Ryan know a thing or two about hockey, hoops, and baseball; but who cares? If the fastball has lost its pop, if the knees don't spring you up after the rebound as quickly as they used to, if the hip check is no longer heavy—then who cares what you "understand"? The message a pro athlete hears is a perversion of what we teach everyone else: Intelligence is less important than pure physical performance.

It is no surprise, then, that athletes tend to shy away from facing the end that approaches. It is no surprise that most of them have to be forced to drop the increasingly futile attempt to play the game, denying up to the last moment that they can't cut it anymore. The fans watch Willie Mays stretch himself out too long and shake their heads at the sad stubbornness; they cluck their tongues when Bernard King, thirty-six years old, having missed the entire previous year with his second season-erasing injury, gets into a fight with his coach because the coach won't assure him he can start every game the minute he returns. Athletes are competitive, proud, and young; you have to drive a stake through their hearts to make most of them stop.

Rivers, however, seems to be fighting the urge to deny that it will end pretty soon. He mentions fairly often that he has only a few years left, and he mentions it always with an assertive, chipper air— as if to assure you (and himself) that he is man enough to face the facts. True, Rivers never talks about ending his playing days without moving directly into his plans to coach. But coaching—or broadcasting, another possibility for Doc—is not the same as playing. And when the chipperness has been established, Rivers is willing also to talk about the pain.

"I know I am going to hurt a lot when I stop playing," he says. "It is going to feel worse than anything I can imagine. I actually cannot anticipate how much I will miss this game—it's too hard to feel in advance. First, there is the game itself. Keep in mind— basketball is not just what I *do;* it is what I *love.* You can't break it down any more than that, you can't say it's the sound of dribbling or sneakers squeaking or huge men going 'Umph!' as they bump each other, you can't pin it down to sights or smells or anything. It's the game itself. The way things open up as soon as the ball starts to move. The way a shot arcs. Man. There is so much."

Rivers shakes his head. "I go back and forth about whether I will ever even play again, just for fun. At the YMCA or something. On the one hand, I cannot imagine not playing ball anymore. There are basketball courts out there, and all I need to do is put on some sneaks and show up, right? But then another part of me makes me feel I won't ever play after I stop playing here, in the NBA. It makes me feel I just won't be able to enjoy anything but this level of the game, this level of competition."

He sighs. "That's what I will miss the most: the competition. It's so challenging, inspiring. It makes you keep moving. It gives you such satisfaction."

For many people who are *not* athletes, competition can be a major pain. It is so *intense*. It distorts natural relationships, heightens pressure, artificially speeds things up. It's safer, more comfy, not to compete.

But to a lot of people—including most, but not all, pro athletes—the chance for victory is worth any potential suffering in defeat. Risking it all makes every moment meaningful; the intensity is not something to fear or avoid, but something to relish with a rowdy grin. To these people any kind of work without competition is pale, slow, lifeless; indeed, given a job in which there is no direct man-on-man fighting, they will create some kind of battle just to keep things interesting.

"I have said before that I am extremely competitive, so much so that it can seem I'm sort of twisted compared to others," says Rivers. "But I have finally figured something out. It is not that I need to beat other people. That is not who I am really competing with, on the deepest level. Other players are just obstacles, challenges put in my way to allow me to prove myself in the ultimate challenge: to play the best I can possibly play. *That* is what I am fighting to do. It is as if there is an ideal inside me of what I can achieve, given my particular talents and limitations. Am I rising to that ideal? Am I getting every last drop out of myself in the effort? Am I fulfilling what it means to be Glenn Rivers and play basketball?"

Rivers describes an inner sense, a kind of intuition, that very sharply lets him know when he is getting the best out of himself and when he is falling short. He says he *always* knows: The inner sense passes judgment with unmistakable clarity. "It comes through loud and clear," he says. "You know without a doubt if you have done your best or quit short. If you haven't done it, sure, you can pretend, you can cover your lack of effort or success, you can cheat any number of ways on your inner count, but you cannot hide from that certainty. The knowledge is there. It is best to face it. Facing the challenge keeps you growing, keeps you moving as a player and a person. Once you begin tricking yourself that you don't hear the voice saying 'Not good enough!' then you begin to accept second best from yourself. After a while, maybe you begin to accept third best. This is the way to go if you want to amount to nothing."

The intuition should be welcomed and trusted and heeded, Rivers says, because it is a gift. When a player chooses to ignore it, the result is very sad. "Nothing is worse than letting yourself down. The most you can hope for in life is to get to a point where you are in charge of your chance for success. Along the way there are lots of circumstances you *can't* control, and sometimes these can bring you down. If you are lucky enough to get through them, and to find yourself in control of your fate, then you'd better take advantage and do everything you can to succeed. If you are lucky enough to get to that point and then you just slacken up—wow. That's a tragedy. I see it happen in the NBA, and there is nothing sadder."

Often no one but the athlete himself has any idea he has fallen short of the best. Sometimes, Rivers says, a player may be a hero to everyone else but knows in himself that he did not play well enough. In the final game of the first round of the 1993 play-offs, the Knicks scrambled back late in the fourth quarter, in a frantic surge powered by some amazing shooting by Rivers, and found themselves in overtime against the Pacers in Indianapolis. While holding the Pacers' best shooter in check on defense, Rivers popped three three-pointers in OT—three threes!—and buried the home team for good. It was his signature game for the season, in the eyes of the media: When the Knicks needed it, he stepped up and took over, hitting the big shots when others could not, stifling Reggie Miller, overcoming a major thumb injury and a habitual disinclination to shoot much. He was the toast of the town.

"But for nearly the whole game I *stank*," he says. "I knew it. My teammates knew it. Pat Riley certainly knew it. I played all but the last five minutes of regulation just *awful*. But then I got hot, and suddenly the game was over, and everyone is crowding around me with a microphone in my face, beaming, expecting me to beam right back, enjoying my big moment. I tried to act like I felt it, but inside I felt stupid. Of course, the main thing was that we won, and nobody was happier about that than me. But as for my personal role in the game—well, I was thinking about how much better I should have played. If I had played halfway decent during the first three quarters, we would not have needed to even go to OT. We would have won easily."

Rivers says this irony happens a lot: A guy is anointed the hero but sits there in the spotlight fretting inside about how much he let the team down. "You can look at guys and tell they feel this way," he says. "And as long as they don't let a personal sulk get in the way of enjoying the team's win, it's good for them to feel a little bad. It shows they're in touch with the main source of competition. It shows they are trying no matter what. There are guys, however, who are too wrapped up in their personal individual story. Sometimes these guys refuse to smile about a win because they didn't play as much as they wanted to, or as well. That's not good. And sometimes—this is the very worst—they will be happy with a loss for the team if they happened to have played a good game. I call this the 'I did all I could do' excuse. It's poisonous."

Rivers recently met a draft choice with good individual statistics for a losing team in college. The kid was excited about getting his chance in the NBA and boasted to Rivers about his numbers. "Did you guys win?" Rivers asked. The player said, "No. We lost a lot." Rivers said, "Then why are you so happy?" The kid shrugged and said, "Well, I did all I could do." Rivers corrected him firmly: "No you didn't. If you had done all you could do, your team would have won. Maybe you should have passed more, allowed another shooter to build his confidence and contribute. Maybe you should have sacrificed some shots for better defense. But there's *something* you should have done. You can't separate yourself that way from the team. Individual victory is not possible in the context of team loss."

There is one last, terrible peril that can befall a player who doesn't heed his intuition about fulfilling his own game: He can try to be something he is not. "The most important thing for any player to learn is, simply, who he is as a basketball player. A player has got to know what he can do and what he cannot. This means acknowledging your strong points and admitting your weak ones. Very few of us are 'complete' ballplayers, equally excellent at every part of the game. I'm certainly not—I am better at some things than others. Facing the facts doesn't mean I stop working to improve my weak points; far from it. But it does mean I don't try to force myself to perform above my head because I think the team needs a certain thing or the coach wants a certain thing. Young players trying to make a team should *never* try to anticipate a coach's desires and match them. A young guy should realize that a coach drafted him or invited him to camp because the coach saw something he liked in that player's natural game. The coach wants him to be himself and contribute his natural strength to the team. If the player tries to be somebody else and provide something else, it can mess up the entire scheme of things."

Rivers mentions a very talented rookie who was drafted by the Atlanta Hawks out of DePaul, a soft-touch finesse forward named Dallas Comegys. Instead of coming to camp and showing the abilities the coaches had picked him for, Comegys decided he needed to show he could be a banger, a rebounder, a tough guy. "He wasted himself," says Rivers. "Instead of floating around and shooting that nice jump shot he had, instead of slicing in on those beautiful quick drives he had shown in college, he was trying to hammer his way beneath the boards, where he had no business. He was getting killed under there. But he had decided he needed to prove something. He was wrong, and all he ended up proving was that he couldn't listen."

Rivers has listened. And not just to that inner sense. His speech is rich with references to other voices, the wisdom and humor of the men he has played with throughout his long career. He mentions so many of them so often, with such alacrity and precise recall, that it's clear he never missed the chance to get close to an interesting teammate. Remembering the topic of retirement, Rivers moves away from considering the competition and instead thinks about the people he has known, sometimes only briefly.

"I guess that's the most precious part," he says. "Teamwork with great people. The chance to work with others. The chance to listen to other guys. I don't want to sound too misty about this, because it's not as if everyone becomes your lifelong buddy. Basketball relationships are more camaraderie than friendship; few of them really grow into durable friendships. That's the way it should be—we all make relatively few great friends in the course of a lifetime, which keeps those friendships special. But the loose kind of camaraderie has a big value too.

"For one thing, camaraderie can be made up of little things and passing encounters. Friendship involves responsibility, even commitment, but many of the guys I remember the best were people I had no chance to develop such things with. For example, I really enjoyed Eric Anderson during his rookie season with the Knicks in 1992–93.

"I spent a year in Atlanta with Gus Williams, a fantastic guard winding up his career. Gus was one of those players who was good enough to have a style all his own. He was so *smooth*, yet so quick. Nobody was better at anticipating passes than Gus—he got a lot of steals by playing the passing lanes just right. He was always The Wizard.

"I really just enjoyed him as a person. I learned a lot from him just by being around him—not from any kind of conscious instruction. Gus was a walking lesson in basketball etiquette. He was neat. He is one of those people I feel I bring a little bit of into play every time I do something. There are several players like that—I do something in a game, and I recognize this player was *there*. It's great. I have been lucky to get to know these guys.

"When I think of that year, I think, 'That year was the Gus year.' It's like that for a lot of my seasons, actually—I think, 'That was the Moses Malone year,' or 'That was the Sidney Moncrief year,' or whatever. It seems as if I always had the chance to get next to somebody who was fun, and interesting, and had a lot to teach."

Rivers will probably always look for opportunities to learn anything useful from anyone. It is this quality—the appreciation of knowledge—that makes him not only a great student of the game but a great teacher. He is modest, almost silent, about his own emergence as a gray eminence whose words are heeded by young guards hanging around *his* locker; he is modest, but also not quite ready to assume the role of the nice-guy veteran "winding up his career." He will mention that Greg Anthony has begun to trust him and ask his advice, especially about defense, or that John Starks looks to him for tips and assurance and steadiness. But mostly he wants to postpone the teacher's role for the next stage of his life, as a coach. He is not a kindhearted old vet helping the kids—not yet. He still has a couple of years left in which to fight them for every minute of playing time. After all, as he says, "Retirement is coming, and I have to face it. But there's no point in rushing things. As long as I can play, as long as the coach thinks I can help the team, I'm *playing*. Try to take my job and you'd better be ready for a battle."

He grins. "That's competition. You can't get away from it."

The Ball

Doc Rivers walks into a Connecticut gymnasium full of sweaty boys and young men wearing shorts, Knicks T-shirts, and hundred-dollar sneakers. His right hand is in a cast from knuckles to mid-forearm, following surgery to repair a severed ligament in his thumb. In the last few minutes of the final game of the 1993 regular season, he took a swipe at the ball as Michael Jordan brought it up from his waist before shooting. ("He does that," Rivers says. "You can knock it away if you're quick.") Just as Rivers swatted, a team-mate bumped him, and his swing went awry. His thumb got caught in the waistband of Jordan's shorts, Jordan jumped up, Rivers, off balance, stumbled to the side, and—r-r-r-rip. He played with no feeling in most of his hand, and no power in his thumb, for the play-offs. ("It didn't hurt my shooting that much," he says, "but I use my thumb a lot in passing. It took something off my chest passes, for sure.")

The boys eye the cast, disappointed. Rivers is spinning a basketball, but they can see it's just a prop. There will be no showtime today—no dribbling exhibition, no jump-shot demo, no underhand-reverse-double-pump-layup fantasia. It's clear Rivers is going to do nothing but *talk*.

Actually, at the start, he's not even going to do that. He's going to make the *boys* do the talking. "If you were going to read a book about basketball," he says, "what would you like to read about?"

It takes at least two-tenths of a second for the kids to overcome their shyness; then the answers pop out, rapid-fire. "Guarding Michael Jordan" is the first, but then they are all mechanics: "Shooting." "Blocking shots." "Position play on defense." "Picks." "Switching." "Jump shots." "Yeah, jump shots." "Passing."

Rivers listens, raising his eyebrows. The call for specific tips is encouraging, it seems; he apparently expected to be asked for more anecdotes ("Tell us about the time you . . ."). He listens until the requests peter out, then asks for a volunteer. A kid in a red Bulls jersey bearing number twenty-three raises his hand, and Rivers calls on him. The kid stands and Rivers sees the shirt. "Hey, *forget it!*" he says with a sardonic laugh, waving the kid down and choosing the guy next to him in a Knicks tee. Everybody laughs, especially the Bulls fan. The volunteer comes out to where Rivers is standing at the foul line.

"Okay," says Doc, holding the ball on his hip. "We are going to play one-on-one, and you can choose one great skill to have: either dribbling or shooting. Which do you choose?"

The kid looks around with an uncertain smile, to see if maybe the other guys think this might be a trick, but then he shrugs and gives a nervous laugh and says, "Shooting, for sure."

"Great!" says Rivers with a cheery smile and a nod. "Then let's start. Come on out here." He walks to a spot about thirty-five feet from the basket, above the top of the key. "Okay, man. Here you go." He hands him the ball, then puts out his arms in classic defensive position and stands right up against him. Suddenly all you can see of the kid is his feet, and he can't move those.

"Hey," says the kid.

"Go ahead," says Doc encouragingly. "Shoot!"

The kid thinks about it, looks around, then just stands there. Rivers steps back, swats him lightly on the hip, and says, "All right, thanks." He turns to the group and says, "See? Everyone in this gym was probably saying the same thing my man here did: 'I want to be a great shooter instead of a great dribbler!' Of course you were—it's the natural thing. But you see what you were doing? You were trying to run before you could walk."

He takes the ball and switches positions with the volunteer. "Now, if I chose dribbling as my great skill, look what I get to do." The kid takes a defensive stance and Rivers throws a minimal head fake. The kid goes back onto his heels for half a second and Rivers, using his left hand, dribbles right around him to a point under the basket.

"Here I am," he says, "where I certainly don't have to be a great shooter to make a bucket." (Somebody in the crowd whispers loudly, "Tell it to Charles Smith!") Rivers sticks the ball back on his hip and thanks the volunteer warmly as the boy sits down, grinning sheepishly. Then he continues the lesson. "Dribbling is like walking. You can't get anywhere without it. And you can get *everywhere* with it. It is the first and most important skill to master. I want you to dribble, with your right hand *and* your left, every second you are on a court—when you're shooting around by yourself, waiting for teams to get picked, playing horse, anything. When you are dribbling, you are practicing your dribble. It's that simple. At first the ball feels like it has a mind of its own and it's kind of pulling against you, it wants to get away, it doesn't like you. You should dribble so much that it feels like the ball *loves* you, wants to stay close and be attached and hang out with you every step. It will happen, believe me. It will become your best friend, so that when you flip it at the floor with every dribble, you know exactly where it is coming back to. Isiah Thomas gives his ball a name, and he talks to it. Really! Every ball he plays with, in practice and in games, he calls by a name. I forget what the name is, but Isiah doesn't let the ball forget: 'You are my buddy,' he says. 'You and I are *tight*.' He talks nicely to that ball. That ball is going to stick around Isiah. Isiah *trusts* that ball."

Rivers holds the ball up. "Look," he says. "Check out this ball.

It is round. It is filled with air. It bounces. Guess what? *All* balls are round. *All* of them are filled with air. They will *all* bounce, exactly the same way. So now that you see it is round, and full of air, you know what? You don't need to look at the ball anymore. Never! No more looking at the ball when you dribble. It is not going to surprise you. You are not going to have to play with a square ball one day. Trust the ball, and keep your eyes *up*. That way you can look at the guys who are open. That way you can see where the defender is, so you don't dribble over him and fall down and let somebody else steal the ball. Here's a good drill for learning not to look at the ball. Anytime you have a ball somewhere around your house or the playground or someplace where there are people, dribble while you carry on a conversation, and make sure you are looking the person you're talking to in the eyes. Make it a good talk, eye to eye. And dribble. That ball is going to be there, where you expect it. Or, if you watch TV and your mom can stand it, dribble while you watch the show. Dribble and read! That's the maximum: dribbling and reading. *That's* concentration." Rivers smiles. "I wish I'd done this more as a kid—especially the *reading* part."

From the emphasis on dribbling, Rivers moves into a basic discussion of offensive play. The kids are sitting up and watching, eyes wide. Anyone who can convince them to get into dribbling over shooting definitely gets their attention.

"When you are playing offense," Doc says, "you have one incredible advantage, and it is enough. Use it well, and this advantage will put the defensive man in a hole he can never climb out of. Does anyone know what this advantage is?"

After a few seconds one kid says tentatively, "You get to move?"

"Right!" Rivers says, nodding appreciatively. "Exactly. You get to make the first move. You get to initiate the play. You get to choose what direction *both* of you are going to go in, and you get to start *ahead* of the man who is guarding you. This is an *awesome* advantage."

He calls another volunteer out of the bunch and stands him in the middle of the foul lane. Facing him, Rivers says, "Okay, here's the drill. We are going to race to one of the lines on the side of the lane here. First man to touch the line with his hand wins. You wait for me to show which line we are racing to. Okay? Ready?" They face each other, arms out. The boy watches Rivers keenly. Rivers darts to the left, and touches the line before the boy has even managed to bend down. They set again, arms out. Rivers darts left again, touches. The boy is pretty quick, but he can never get started before Rivers touches a line. They do the drill six times, and Rivers pats him on the back and sits him down.

"You see?" he says. "I was *in charge*. I had an unbeatable advantage. A great player never wastes it, never lets his defender recover. The best man I ever saw at using this was Larry Bird. People will tell you Larry Bird was big and slow and dull and couldn't jump. They say all he could do was shoot jump shots. Boy, are they wrong. Larry Bird had the best first step of anybody I know. When he faced you, he knew exactly *what* he was going to do, and exactly *when*, and you didn't. You knew nothing; you could only wait on Larry. And, by the way, his first step was pretty quick. Not super-quick, but because he made it at the right moment, and because it was so decisive, it looked all the quicker. Once Larry Bird had made that first step, he didn't *have* to be fast anymore. He could be as slow and dull as he wanted, because you were behind him and he was six ten and he could shoot whatever kind of little shot he wanted without you bothering him in the least. After that first step, you were out of the picture."

Standing there under the basket, Rivers holds up a warning finger. "*But*. But there is an instance in which Larry Bird's first step would not be enough, when he *would* have to be fast in order to keep his advantage. Can anybody think of what that is?" Nobody can. Rivers takes a couple of steps away from the basket, so that he is standing just outside the paint.

"Larry Bird started his move *here*." He faces the basket.

Looking at it, holding the ball with both hands, he goes on. "If he gets that first-step advantage in here, and a quicker man is guarding him, as we have seen, the man has no chance to catch up." He makes a quick move and with one dribble he has a layup. He retrieves the ball and walks out past the foul line, past the top of the key. "But what if Larry Bird makes his nasty first step out here?" He faces the basket, makes a move, and takes six dribbles, stopping just short of a layup spot. "Well, then Larry Bird has given his defender all this space"—he waves at the floor behind him—"and all those dribbles to catch up. Or he has given all that time for another man to slide over and cover him." He turns, ball on hip, and points at the boys. "So remember: It's not just that you make a good first step. It's also that you choose the right spot to start from. Pick a spot that will allow you to finish your play without the man catching up."

One of the camp directors, standing at the rear of the group, signals Rivers: He has a few minutes left. The boys have to go eat lunch. They don't look like they would ever care about eating again as long as Rivers stayed out there opening their eyes this way. And he seems as if he could stay there forever too: This kind of teaching is obviously right in the middle of his heart. But this isn't his camp, and he is not a coach yet— he's a guest speaker with forty minutes of someone else's kids' attention. So he begins to quicken his tips.

"Basketball is a simple game," he says. "If you do several simple things very well and stick with them, you will be good. You make it simple, and keep it simple. You do your good things over and over. This is one reason Pat Riley made our defense so good last season: He found the simple way we played best, and he told us to play that way every night. Over and over. So we mastered those skills, all together."

Rivers spins the ball, then cradles it and steps closer to the kids. "There are two last things I want to tell you. One is, don't let anybody talk you out of your personal dream. Whatever your dream is—whether it is playing in the NBA or being a doctor or having a big family or getting a Ph.D. If you are lucky enough to know what you want, don't give up on it. Plenty of people have no idea what they want; they go through life waiting for it to happen to them. If you *know*, then *get* it. Don't let someone say you shouldn't want it, don't let someone try to substitute a goal he or she thinks is right.

"When I was in the fourth grade, we did this thing in class about goals and life. The teacher made each of us come up and write a sentence on the board, saying what we wanted. When it was my turn, I went up and I wrote, "I want to be a pro basketball player.' Then I sat down. The teacher immediately gave me a lecture, gave the whole class a lecture based on my 'mistake.' She said, 'This is the wrong kind of thing to write. Why? Because Glenn is not being *realistic*.' She asked me to go up and write something realistic. I went back up. I intended to write something better. But I wrote, 'I want to be a pro basketball player.' "

Rivers shakes his head. "Man, that teacher went *crazy*. She got so mad, she kicked me right out of the class, sent me to the principal, and he suspended me. Sent me home. Well, it just so happens my father was at home. My father the policeman. I got home, and he said, 'What are you doing here?' I told him. He said, 'The principal called me from school. He said you aren't showing respect for your teacher.' I said, 'I was just telling the truth. I don't have to respect her so much I lie to her, do I?' He said, 'Your teacher knows more about the world than you do. You have to believe her when she tells you something isn't realistic. Now come on—we're going back to that classroom. You are going to do the right thing.' And he walked with me back to school. Walked with me down the hall, walked into the classroom with me. The teacher looked up, all shocked, afraid. 'My son wants to write his goal on the board again,' he said. He nodded to me. 'Go.' So I went to the board. I picked up the chalk. I did the right thing."

He sighs. "I wrote, 'I want to be a pro basketball player.' Then I looked at my teacher, and at my father. He stared at me, hard. Then, after a long time, he looked over at my teacher, who was waiting for him to say something. 'I guess that's what he wants,' he said. 'I guess that's the truth, I guess that's *realistic*, for him.' Then he left. When I got home, he took me aside. 'If you're going to stand up for something like that,' he said, 'make sure you stick with it.' "

Rivers raises a hand. "Sticking with it does not just mean continuing to want it. It means *working* to get it. Once you decide what you want, the days of just 'wanting' are over. It's time to start working. My coach Andrew Johnson asked me what my goal was once, and I told him, same thing I wrote on the board, and he laughed. 'So what?' he said. 'Every kid in the country wants to be a pro ballplayer. What makes you different?' He said, 'There's a kid in Jersey wants to be in the NBA. There's a kid in California. In Kansas. In Florida. So how are you going to rise above these guys?' He told me to think about these kids out there, and to realize that if I was sitting around in Chicago shooting the breeze with the boys, or watching TV, or spinning the ball on my finger, maybe that kid in Jersey was *dribbling*. Maybe the kid in Florida was *shooting free throws*. While I'm goofing off. And when that kid and I compete for a spot at rookie camp, that kid has outworked me and he will beat me out of a job."

Rivers shakes his head. "Never let anybody beat you by out-working you. If he's more talented, or luckier on that day, and you have both worked the same, then there's no disgrace in him beating you. But if he beats you because he simply worked harder—well, then how are you going to live with yourself? If he did something you could just as easily have done but *didn't*, then you have let yourself down. You have thrown away a chance."

A common way to throw away a chance, Rivers says, is by accepting excuses. "There are lots of excuses for falling short. Every kid has them. Black kids in particular have them. 'He has more money than me,' or 'He went to a better school,' or 'His parents work with him,' or 'His parents drive him to practice and I have to walk,' or 'He gets the breaks.' " Rivers nods. So do several kids. "*Good* excuses. *True* excuses. *Excellent* reasons for failing.

We've all thought them, because they *do* seem to explain a lot. But you have to resist using an excuse. A bad break can slow you down, but it cannot stop you. Only you can stop you. An excuse is just an excuse. And let me tell you—you'll find a coulda-been-a-star player on every playground, using them to explain why he never made it. It's always someone else's fault, man."

The camp director signals Rivers again; Rivers nods. "And now a final point. When I was a senior in high school, I was one of the top two recruits in the United States, according to various ranking services. The other was Derek Harper, a guard out of Florida, who has had a great career in Dallas after going to Illinois. Every college program you could think of was offering me scholarships; I had coaches, grown men, begging me to come to their school, pleading with me, offering me every kind of illegal inducement, saying their jobs depended on getting me, all this pressure—it was incredible. Derek had the same, I'm sure. Now, I'm not telling you this to brag, to make you think of what a big guy I was—I am telling you because I have a surprising thing to say. You know what? I was not even the best player *on my high-school team.*"

Rivers lets it sink in. "Do you hear me? I was maybe the top prospect in the country, but not even the top guy on my own team in Maywood, Illinois. Because there was a kid just as good as I was, as good as Isiah, as good as anyone. An awesome player. A player who could do anything with a basketball, who could make all the people in the gym, on both teams and in the stands, hold their breath anytime he wanted. But this guy thought being good with a ball was all he needed to worry about. So he let everybody flatter him, and he expected to be able to take whatever he wanted out of life, anything, from anybody. Basketball was the shortcut to the top. No one could stop him on the court, so no one could stop him anywhere.

"I was getting all this attention, but I noticed no one was recruiting this other player. So I finally asked a coach why nobody seemed interested in him. It was Ray Meyer of DePaul, who at the time was probably the most experienced, smartest, most careful coach in the country, the guy who had seen it all twenty times. I asked him why he wasn't going after the guy. He said, kind of cautiously, 'Well, there's some bad feeling about that kid.' I pressed him: 'Rumors? Or stuff somebody knows?' He was still careful, but he was being straight with me, and said, 'Well, some people say things, about drugs, about some possible trouble with the law. But it's not really the rumors. I just feel things aren't right with him. He is not a good bet.'

"I was a little upset. I thought this was kind of unfair. But it turned out Coach Meyer's feeling was right. This guy got busted. And busted again, and again. Drugs, theft, guns. It all fell in on him. I went to college, but he went to jail. For a *long* time. Where his basketball talent did him no good at all."

Rivers pauses. "A few years ago, I visited this guy. He had figured things out by then. He knew what had happened. He was not one of those criminals who turn bitter and decide they are victims of the brutal system, and feel sorry for themselves forever. Quite the contrary. He told me, 'Look, man, this is all my own fault. I made all the choices, and they were bad ones. I got nobody to blame but me.' Then he shook his head, and smiled, and sighed. 'The thing is, man—I had my chance. That's all any person can ask for. I could have used what I had, and gone on. I didn't need anything more. But I blew it, I threw it away. I got to live with that.' "

Rivers looks around the gym. "Each of you is going to get your chance. You were *born* with your chance. When it comes, take it. Take it *smart*. And for the rest of your life, enjoy yourself."

Rivers puts the ball quietly down on the court and looks at it. So does everyone else. The ball seems too still; there is something alarming about a basketball alone and unmoving. Seen like this, it is just one round object, and when one thinks about this thing as the repository of so many dreams, so much pressure, so much misplaced swagger and daring and power, one feels the urge to think again. One feels the need to look elsewhere for the grace and determination and wit that a basketball life contains: not to look to the ball for them, but to look within oneself. Perhaps this is what Rivers intends by putting the ball down, and glancing at it significantly. Hey. That's just a ball.

Index

About the Coauthor

Bruce Brooks is the author of an unbroken string of critically acclaimed novels and nonfiction books for young readers, among them *What Hearts* and *The Moves Make the Man*. His most recent book, *Boys Will Be*, was published by Holt.